How Schools Can Help Combat

Child
Abuse and
Neglect

The Advisory Panel

More than 500 educators reviewed the original manuscript of *Child Abuse and Neglect*. Space prohibits the listing of each participant. However, the author expresses her appreciation for the revisions and suggestions they contributed.

The Author

Cynthia Crosson Tower is Associate Professor in the Human Services Program, Behavioral Science Department, at Fitchburg State College in Massachusetts. Dr. Tower has worked with the Massachusetts Department of Social Services in the Adoption Placement Unit, Protective Services, Family and Children's Services; and has had extensive experience in writing and conducting training programs about child abuse and neglect. She acts as a consultant on the subject for schools and social workers, and is the developer of the NEA Child Abuse and Neglect Training Program. A licensed Independent Clinical Social Worker, Dr. Tower also maintains a private practice specializing in incest survivors.

How Schools Can Help Combat

Child Abuse and Neglect

Second Edition

by Cynthia Crosson Tower

nea PROFESSIONAL LIBRARY

National Education Association
Washington, D.C.

Printing History:
  FirstPrinting: March 1984
  Second Printing: July 1984
  Third Printing: February 1985
  SECOND EDITION: March 1987

Library of Congress Cataloging-in-Publication Data

Tower, Cynthia Crosson.
  How schools can help combat child abuse and neglect.

  (How schools can help combat series)
  Updated ed. of: Child abuse and neglect. c1984.
  Bibliography: p.
  1. Child abuse—United States.   2. Child abuse—Law
and legislation—United States.   3. Teacher-student
relationships—United States.   I. Tower, Cynthia
Crosson. Child abuse and neglect.   II. Title.
III. Series.
HV6626.5.T68 1987   362.7'044   86–31232
ISBN 0-8106-3296-9
ISBN 0-8106-3295-0 (pbk.)

To

Chay, Jamie,

and

Fenneke

The NEA Policy on Child Abuse and Neglect

NEA Resolution

B–37. Child Abuse/Exploitation

The National Education Association believes that all children should be protected from any form of child abuse and/or exploitation and that all school personnel are in a position to observe and recognize abuse that has been inflicted on children. The Association deplores media exploitation, commercialization, and glamorization of physical, emotional, or sexual child abuse.

The Association and its affiliates should—

a. Cooperate with community organizations to increase public awareness and understanding of child abuse

b. Encourage the development and use of materials to increase student awareness of child abuse

c. Encourage development of preparation courses and professional development programs for all school personnel that stress the identification of, reporting procedures for, and techniques in dealing with abused children

d. Encourage the development by affiliates of educator awareness programs dealing with the abused child.

The Association and its affiliates urge the enactment of federal, state, and local legislation that would—

a. Provide school personnel reporting suspected child abuse immunity from legal action

b. Require school personnel to report to the appropriate authorities instances of suspected child abuse/exploitation

c. Provide due process for school personnel accused of child abuse/exploitation while performing their duties

d. Provide for protection of children from other children. (74, 85)

CONTENTS

Contents

Foreword

Some teachers are uncertain about the significance of the clues. Other teachers make accurate diagnoses but may not know what to do. Those who know, often are afraid to act. This book by Cynthia Crosson Tower will help overcome these problems. She demystifies the social, psychological, and legal aspects of child abuse and neglect. After reading this book, teachers will find the mechanics of detection and reporting to be very clear.

I would be proud to report that schools of education, or most schools of education, or even my own school of education, adequately prepare teachers to recognize these problems and to act effectively. I cannot make this claim. Schools of education are overburdened preparing teachers to instruct in the "basics," to solve other problems, or simply to survive teaching. But truly, is there anything more basic than helping to stop the destruction of children's bodies and the warping of their minds?

According to the psychoanalyst Erik Erikson, "the worst sin is the mutilation of a child's spirit." Abuse and neglect of children are heinous not only because youngsters are vulnerable and relatively powerless, but also because the effects of such maltreatment are so deep, so broad, and so long-lasting. As a clinical psychologist, I work with these victims of abuse and neglect as adults. Thirty years after being sexually abused as a four-year-old, one female client is still unable to relate meaningfully to men, has recurrent nightmares and heavy residues of anger and shame. Another client, who was physically abused as a child, married an abuser, but sought help only after his beatings extended beyond her to their children. This cycle may continue for generations. One neglected child years later completed her training as a nurse. Her professional competence is balanced by an equal and opposite homelife. Her nearly pathological tantrums, filthy home, jealousy, and infidelity are stunting her children's growth, destroying her marriage, and making her own consciousness hellish. Helping to stop child abuse and neglect simultaneously contains the long-term human costs, like spotting and stopping a contagious disease before it becomes an epidemic.

Dr. Tower's book authoritatively and realistically fills a gap in the information available to teachers. The rest is up to us. We need to use the information well, so that our students have a chance to become wholesome adults. Helping to stop child abuse and neglect is a courageous act of love.

—Alfred Alschuler
Professor of Education
University of Massachusetts

Preface

This book is dedicated to all school employees, in recognition of their attempts to provide the best possible education for children. I have tried to answer the questions that teachers most often ask about recognizing abuse, neglect, and sexual abuse, and the necessity and logistics of reporting.

In many instances, the nature of the material requires the use of clinical, biological terms. It is essential to be specific so that all who are concerned about these issues can understand exactly what is involved. It is also important to speak clearly and realistically about the nature of these problems, avoiding euphemisms or evasions, in order to deal with them and work toward prevention.

In addition, I have attempted to give a picture not only of the abusive or neglectful parent, but also of the social service system that acts upon the report made by the educator. As a social worker turned educator, it is my feeling that the teacher and the social worker are invaluable to each other in their mutual goal—enhancing the child's chances for a healthy development. During my years as a protective social worker, I realized the importance of the teacher's role in maltreatment situations—from initial detection to further validation to later assistance in treatment efforts through classroom activities to prevention. Now, as a teacher, I continue to work with social workers to strengthen the bond of these two professions. This book is another attempt to do so.

I would like to recognize the assistance and support of the many who made this book possible. The members of the Review Board who took time to write letters and suggest revisions based upon their own experiences and frustrations have made this undertaking more comprehensive.

I am especially indebted to Muriel Crosson for her encouragement as well as for her excellent editing and typing. My husband, Charles, and my children have been patient and have given me a great deal of support in this venture, for which I am very grateful. I would also like to thank those mentors who have encouraged and believed in me— Marianne Micks, Carel Germaine, and Al Alschuler. Finally, I do not believe any such work would have been possible had it not been for my teacher in writing and in life, James Cope Crosson.

—Cynthia Crosson Tower

14

Introduction to
the Second Edition

Several years ago when a handbook for school employees was being considered, there was a recognition that many teachers felt unsure about how to recognize and report abuse and neglect. These teachers felt that they had never had an abused or neglected child in their classroom, only to discover, after becoming better informed, that they may have had more such children than they realized at the time. In the first edition I suggested that teachers must learn more about maltreatment and participate in combating the problem for several reasons.

First, the trauma and residual effects of abuse and neglect can be as detrimental to a child's ability to learn as are the perceptual difficulties that schools spend so much time addressing today. Only through relief of the pressure placed upon the child by the abuse or neglect can significant learning take place.

Second, school employees have daily contact with children. Classroom teachers, especially, see the child in a variety of situations and may be privy to some of the most intimate information about the child's life. Not only do teachers have more contact with a child than other adults—except the caretaker—but they also have a tremendous amount of influence on the developing youngster. They are in an excellent position to help the child deal with concerns that are barriers to learning.

And third, in all states teachers and other school personnel are mandated by law to report suspected child abuse and neglect; they can in fact be held liable for failure to do so.

Originally I suggested that teachers may not be reporting because they do not feel comfortable about their ability to recognize abuse and neglect; they may find it difficult to believe or convince others of their findings; or they may not know how or to whom to report the abuse.

Since the publication of the first edition of this book, the picture has changed. Social service agencies report that more teachers are calling in their concerns about abused children. School systems are providing training to help their employees more accurately recognize maltreatment. And children are more aware of the teacher as a concerned ally to whom they can go with this haunting secret. Teachers who are armed with knowledge and confidence feel more powerful as part of the vital team to help abused and neglected children. The concern of many teachers now is, "What can *I* do to help in the *prevention* of child abuse and neglect?"

Before considering this question in depth, let us think about what is meant by prevention:

> Preventive intervention can take place at any of three different points in time: before the phenomenon has ever occurred; before it has occurred to a serious degree (but after certain warning signals have appeared); and after it has occurred, to keep it from recurring. It can also take place between these points on the continuum. (23, pp.1–2)*

The preventive tools used in the classroom can address all three of these points on the continuum. In fact, preventive intervention through schools can be the most effective type of prevention.

This second edition is dedicated to the phenomenon of prevention. Throughout, it provides school employees with information to refer to— such as the symptoms of abuse and neglect, how to validate suspected abuse and neglect, how to report abuse and neglect, and how to understand the maltreating parent. It also addresses fundamental questions about prevention as well. Teachers ask, "How can I introduce prevention in my classroom?" With the current abundance of prevention materials, they wonder, "How do I know what are effective, safe,

---

*Numbers in parentheses appearing in the text refer to the Bibliography beginning on page 221.

prevention tools to use?" This book tries to answer all these questions.

Recently I gave a workshop for teachers on preventing child sexual abuse. Amidst a flurry of questions, one frustrated teacher stood up and said, "Why can't we just forget about this stuff! We're teaching kids things they don't need to know. My teachers never taught me anything about being abused and I'm fine." A hush fell over the audience as the man sat down, sure his point was well taken. All eyes turned to me expectantly, but before I could respond a woman in the back row stood up— unnoticed until then.

"May I say something?" she asked quietly. "At six I was molested by my own father. I assumed all fathers treated their children that way. He beat me too, but no one seemed to notice the marks he left when I went to school. No one seemed to notice how unhappy I was. I especially liked my third grade teacher and I tried to tell her. I wrote notes and left them for her. I don't think it occurred to her that that kind of thing could happen. She was a good teacher and a concerned person, but she couldn't hear my cry for help. My mother wouldn't listen either. I knew after that it was useless to try to tell anyone. It never occurred to me that I could say no—that my body was my own. The abuse continued until I was married at 17—and it has hurt me in so many ways since." By now the woman's voice had risen in volume, and she spoke clearly and with emotion. "I want my children to know they have choices. I want them to know they have rights and that no one can hurt them. I want them to know that there are knowledgeable people whom they can go to and who will believe them. I tell them that, but I want others to tell them too!" After a pause, she continued, "Now I'm a teacher and I want to be part of teaching children to protect themselves as well as to learn." She took a deep breath, then sat down. There was silence; then the sound of applause came from two or three sections of the audience. Within a few seconds the whole room resounded with support.

INTRODUCTION

That day, that instance was a powerful lesson on the need for neglect and abuse prevention. The teacher's appeal presented a challenge, too—to teach children and remove all the barriers to their learning, no matter what the barriers might be. We can do this by understanding, believing, and reporting, as well as empowering children to protect themselves. It is a challenge well within our grasp.

Not only teachers and past victims recognize the need for prevention. New research, especially in the area of sexual abuse, tells us that the abuse of children *can* be prevented.

Recently David Finkelhor of the University of New Hampshire Family Violence Program created a precondition model based upon his years of research in child sexual abuse. He theorizes that four preconditions must exist before a perpetrator can sexually abuse a child. The first two rest with individuals: why they are motivated to abuse children and why their own internal inhibitors do not prevent them from abusing. The last two preconditions are concerned with (a) the external inhibitors or roadblocks that parents or society set up to prevent the abuse from happening, and (b) the abuser's overcoming the child's resistance to cooperating (18, pp. 53–61).

How can prevention serve to block the existence of these preconditions? First, public awareness about abuse and neglect helps parents and teachers as well to recognize their need to better supervise children. For example, a prison inmate serving time for the sexual assault of children once said that schools built in secluded areas and immediately surrounded by woods give the child molester or adbuctor a perfect opportunity to drag or coax a child into the woods undetected. While the architects and planners of such schools may consider the aesthetic and natural beauty of such a setting, the child molesters use the area for their own ends. By knowing this, those who supervise children at school can do so more conscientiously. At home, informed parents can choose babysitters more carefully, and

18

they can be alert to any clues that family members may exhibit by behaving strangely, or that a child may exhibit by becoming withdrawn and/or secretive.

Prevention also empowers children to protect themelves. Those who are assertive and who learn to say no will not be easy prey for the child molester. Children who recognize that what began as a fun-filled tickling game has become frightening can respect their feelings and tell the tickler to stop, or they can tell someone else. Whether a victim of sexual abuse or physical abuse, children who are taught that they have a right not to be hurt will be better able to ask for help. Part of prevention is teaching children not only *how* to recognize that they are being exploited, abused, or neglected, but also *whom* to tell when they feel in need of help. Such information broadens children's conceptions of the resources available and may help them in other instances as well.

Despite progress in prevention efforts, however, there is a need for improvement. Attempts in the classroom to date, although a start, are inadequate in several areas. Prevention should cover all types of abuse and neglect, not only sexual abuse. In the case of *physical abuse—*

1. We need to teach children that hitting is not the answer. Teaching them to express anger verbally rather than demonstrate it by striking out may not only help them to be nonabusing parents, but it may also help them to recognize this behavior in their parents.

2. We need to help children identify when they are under stress. Once they recognize the cause of their stress, they will be better equipped to seek ways to alleviate the cause.

3. We need to teach children problem solving. Abuse is about feeling out of control. The ability to tackle problems and make decisions gives children more tools to keep feeling in control as they mature and face other problems.

For *neglect—*

1. We need to teach children about being adults— from budgeting to holding a job to being a parent. We frequently give them the theory, but forget even the rudimentary how-tos until they are faced with learning by experience.

2. We need to teach children that their bodies are wonderful machines that can work for them. If these machines are not cared for—cleaned, fed, and kept free of addictive substances—they will not perform at their best.

For *sexual abuse—*

1. We need to teach normal sexuality along with abnormal. In other words, sexual abuse prevention should be part of a total look at sexuality from anatomy to reproduction. The message should be—here's the way things should be or could be—and—this is what can go wrong. Teaching children *only* about the abusive elements of sexuality will give them a distorted message.

2. We must empower children to say no when it becomes necessary. Children need to know their rights as well as their responsibilities. They need to know why they must do some things adults tell them to do—that *usually* those things are to help them become responsible adults. Such an approach may necessitate examining our own values and practices. An authoritarian approach that says, "Do what I say because I say it!" while telling children to say no to sexual abuse sends a mixed message. We need to let children know that cleaning their room and helping around the house prepares them to be worthwhile adults. They also need to know that a degree of quiet in the classroom helps the teacher present the lesson so that everyone can benefit. In contrast, being molested or beaten by an adult is not preparation for adulthood.

Prevention is about stopping abuse now and knowing where to get help; it is also about growing up to be a good and nonabusive parent. The preceding instructional suggestions can help children achieve these goals.

But prevention has another side. It need not be only in the classroom. Prevention for schools means teachers educated not only in increased awareness in the classroom, but in the community as well. Prevention means having a voice in lobbying against pornography, which has been found to greatly stimulate the potential sexual offender (18). Prevention means being involved in the movement to decrease the amount of violence and suggestive advertising on television.

School employees have a responsibility to support programs that help parents become more effective in their job. There are a variety of ways that school personnel can make a real impact in the area of preventing child abuse. As the reports to child protective agencies increase daily, our efforts at prevention must also increase. Only then can we hope to make a significant difference.

This book is about prevention—about arming ourselves with the knowledge to recognize and report abuse, but with the intent that for the next child *we* may be there before the abuse happens, so that the child may have protected him/herself by saying no or telling someone before it was too late. What a wonderful feeling to know that *we* made the difference.

CHAPTER 1

How to Recognize Physical and Emotional Abuse and Neglect

•

A breathless, harried high school teacher greeted me as I arrived to conduct in-service training on abuse and neglect for a group of local teachers.

"I'm so glad you're here!" he breathed, and then proceeded to recount his day's activity attempting to report a suspected case of abuse of a 14-year-old student.

"I shouldn't have waited so long, but I just wasn't sure and didn't know whom to tell!" He had finally told the school nurse, and for the rest of the day, he and she had tried to contact the appropriate agency. Feeling that it was his duty to do so, he had also told the mother of his intent. The mother, fearful of her abusive husband, had picked up the child and fled. Now after hours, the confused teacher was left not knowing whom to go to, not knowing if the child was in danger, and agonizing over his role in the entire matter.

•

It became painfully obvious to me as I tried to help this teacher—to identify the proper agency to which to make the report and to elicit a promise from social services that the case would be treated as an emergency—that he might well exemplify the plight of many teachers when they are faced with one of society's most difficult problems. I considered how many other educators would benefit from the knowledge of exactly what to do in such a crisis situation.

Concerned teachers are not only confronted with possible physical abuse of children;* they may also encounter physical neglect, emotional abuse, and sexual abuse as well. This chapter examines physical and emotional abuse and neglect. Chapter 2 deals with sexual abuse.

Physical Abuse

Physical abuse refers to a nonaccidental physical injury to a child. The most obvious way to detect it is by outward physical signs such as the following:

- extensive bruises, especially numerous bruises of different colors, indicating various stages of healing (strange bruises are always possible in normal activities; it is their frequency that arouses suspicions of abuse)

  Ages of bruises can be approximately detected by the following colors:

    Immediate–few hours = red
    6–12 hours = blue
    12–24 hours = black-purple
    4–6 days = green tint, dark
    5–10 days = pale green to yellow (13, p.8)*

- burns of all types (although burns may also be accidental), but especially glove-like burns, which indicate that the hand has been immersed in hot liquid; burns that are more intense in the middle and radiate from there, which could indicate that hot liquid has been poured onto the skin; cigarette burns; burns in the shape of an object such as a poker, an iron

- bruises in specific shapes such as handprints, hanger marks

- frequent complaints of soreness or awkward movements, as if caused by pain

---

*Child or children as used in this book (unless otherwise defined) refers to any person(s) under 18 years of age.

- marks that indicate hard blows from an object such as an electrical cord or other whiplike object that could make a burn around the body
- bruises on multiple parts of the body indicating blows from different directions
- unexplained abdominal swelling (may be caused by internal bleeding)
- extreme sensitivity to pain
- frequent bruises around the head or face (the area of other bruises may be important—knees and elbows, for example, are especially vulnerable in normal falls; bruises to the abdomen or midway between the wrist and elbow may be more unlikely in normal activities)
- bald spots indicative of severe hair pulling.

The key thing to look for in physical abuse is an explanation that does not fit the injury. For example, the child reports a "fall" while the bruises indicate the clear outline of an object such as a belt, or the child who "fell off the bed" is too severely bruised for such a fall.

Behaviorally, children also give many clues.

•

Kara, age 5, always presented a neat, well-ordered picture. Although not expensive, her clothes were well-chosen, clean, and pressed. Her long-sleeved blouses and colorful tights seemed a bit strange in warmer weather, but the teacher made no comments about them. The child was very affectionate, almost to the point of smothering; her endearing ways made her an easy candidate for teacher's pet. It was not until Kara unexplainably wet her pants and the teacher helped her remove her tights to clean up, that anything seemed amiss. Kara's small legs revealed numerous bruises in various stages of healing. An examination by the school nurse attested to the abuse Kara had suffered over her entire body.

•

Joe was not a difficult child, nor was he unlikable. He was just "there" in the classroom of 30 other bubbling,

24

boisterous youngsters. He did his work as instructed and never talked back. His only problem was frequently falling asleep. Joe's "accidents"—the bruises in September, the broken arm in January, and the burned hands in March— did not even raise the teacher's suspicions. When the teacher made a special effort to talk with apparently shy Joe, the story came out. He had been abused by his mother for several years.

•

Kevin, a boisterous, unruly, and pugnacious child, spent a good deal of time sitting in the assistant principal's office. Most of the teachers at the junior high school dreaded his appearance in class. In the past year he had run away from home. In fact, his biggest fear was that the school would call his home. It was not until the school received word from the local social service agency that Kevin had been removed from his home due to life-threatening abuse, that the cause of his behavior became more apparent.

•

The three preceding vignettes depict examples of reactions that children may exhibit to abuse. Kara's story speaks of a well-ordered home where expectations run high. Her desire to please within this rigid framework transfers itself to school as well. Joe's behavior is probably indicative of the most prolonged, severe abuse. Here is a child who has turned inward, who may spend his nighttime hours wakeful, fearing more abuse, and his daytime hours fighting his body's need for sleep. He describes himself as accident-prone, protecting the homelife he is convinced he deserves.

While the problems of Kara and Joe may go unnoticed by some, Kevin's problem is more obvious. Kevin is striking out at the world, which appears to give him nothing but abuse. He is at the hub of an ever-moving wheel of abuse and misperception. At home he is beaten by an alcoholic father who spends his sober hours expounding the virtues of machismo. His attempts to cry for help in school translate into disruptive behavior and meet with more rejection. If his parents are called in, the cycle repeats itself.

Behaviorally, there are a number of ways to recognize the abused child. Kara, Joe, and Kevin exemplify several characteristics:

- overcompliance
- withdrawal, perpetual sleepiness
- acting out, aggressive, disruptive behavior.

Other behavioral symptoms to consider are

- destructiveness to self and others
- coming to school too early or leaving late—a clear indicator of fear of going home
- cheating, stealing, or lying (this may be related too high expectations at home)
- accident proneness (ruling out organic problems, such behavior may be unconsciously self-destructive; if the accidents are "reported" but do not happen at school, it may be a coverup for abuse)
- fearfulness (the child may assume that adults hurt and is constantly on guard)
- low achievement (in order to learn, children must convert aggressive energy into learning; children who are either overly aggressive or lacking in energy may have little or no energy for learning)
- inability to form good peer relationships (many abusive parents prohibit their child from seeking out friends, perhaps because of fear of exposure)
- wearing clothing that covers the body and that may be inappropriate for warm months
- dislike of or shrinking from physical contact (the child may not tolerate physical praise such as a pat on the back)
- regressiveness, exhibiting less mature behavior. (See Appendix A for a quick reference chart of physical and behavioral indicators.)

These symptoms apply to adolescents as well as to younger children. The abuse of adolescents is also a major problem, although many do not recognize it as such for several reasons:

1. Adolescents do not fit the picture of child victims.

2. Adolescents may have as much strength or weight as adults.

3. Adolescents may be provocative (physically, verbally, or sexually).

4. Adolescents seem capable of better impulse control than younger children.

5. Adolescents may be perceived as able to run away from or avoid an abusive situation.

6. Adolescents may appear to have access to more potential help (such as police or social services) outside the family. (19, p. 18)

Despite the apparent advantages of adolescents over younger children, in an abusive situation they are still hampered by ties and remnants of family dependence from childhood. Adolescents need to be seen as independent, but their history has probably been one of returning to the family for safety. They may also have come to believe that any fault lies with them rather than with the family.

In addition to the symptoms noted, which are obvious in younger children, certain behavioral indicators, although perhaps true of younger children, are seen especially in adolescents. Abuse is suspect in adolescents who—

• overreact to being touched in any way (react with fear or aggression).

• seem to provoke encounters of abusive treatment from adults as well as from peers.

• demonstrate extremes in behavior—either great hostility and aggressiveness or withdrawal.

• exhibit assaultive, aggressive, or pugnacious behavior.

• appear to be overly frightened of parents.

• act out continually or are described as incorrigible. (19, p. 13)

When considering adolescent abuse, the school is decidedly the *most* important link in the helping chain. The teacher is the professional *most* likely to detect abuse in this age group and is in the best position to report. Younger children may come to the attention of members of the medical profession; as a rule, abused teens do not.

Keep in mind, however, that observing one or two of these symptoms in any age group does not *necessarily* mean abuse. It does mean that you should be watchful—carefully observing the child for additional indicators. Many of the factors mentioned may be indicative of other problems as well. In addition, there are cultural factors to consider. For example, some Vietnamese children may suffer from unusual bruises around the head and neck resulting from common folk remedies for headaches or colds. Long-sleeved shirts or pants worn by Moslem girls may be a custom rather than a response to the weather or a coverup for abuse. Documenting strange or unusual behavior can help the unsure teacher accumulate a variety of clues and perhaps become aware of an abusive pattern.

Remember that emotionally, physical abuse affects children in many ways. Victims suffer from poor self-image, feelings of little self-worth and, perhaps, that they deserve the abuse. In addition, they may have learned that adults will hurt them; therefore they are watchful and untrusting. Children reflect their family life. Those who present a negative, depressed picture may well be mirroring the unrest at home—if not actual abuse, certainly some other kind of family disturbance.

Physical Neglect

Physical neglect refers to the failure on the part of the caretaker to meet the child's basic physical needs.

●

My first impression of Robbie was of the dull appearance of his hair and eyes. Somehow this was even more striking than the odor emanating from his corner desk. Sullen and quiet, Robbie drifted through my first grade lessons, barely able to find a pencil in his disorganized desk. His lunch usually consisted of Twinkies, which he said he bought on his walk to school. Later I learned that he more frequently stole them from the corner store. He eyed the other children's lunches covetously, and once I saw him steal an apple when a classmate turned her back. Quickly, like a furtive animal, he thrust the apple into the pocket of his dirty, faded, tattered pants.

Notes and phone calls to his parents met with no response. Robbie was a sad little nomad, drifting into school and listlessly returning home, reportedly to take care of his younger brother and sister.

●

Robbie is not unlike many other neglected children. Teachers often remark upon their general dull appearance. In addition, these victims of neglect—

- may appear in soiled clothing, significantly too small or too large and often in need of repair.

- always seem to be hungry, hoarding or stealing food but coming to school with little of their own.

- may appear listless and tired.

- often report caring for younger siblings, when the child caretaker may be only 5, 6, 7, or 8.

- demonstrate poor hygiene, may smell of urine, or have bad breath or dirty teeth (although inconsistent bathing may be in vogue for teenagers, this practice should be distinguishable from the condition of the chronically unbathed, unkempt child).

- have unattended medical or dental problems such as infected sores or badly decayed or abscessed teeth.

- may have lice.

- may exhibit stealing, vandalism, or other delinquent behavior.

- may have frequent school absences or tardiness.
- have poor peer relationships, perhaps because of hygienic problems or a depressed, negative attitude.
- may be withdrawn.
- may crave affection, even eliciting negative responses to accomplish it.
- may be destructive or pugnacious, showing no apparent guilt over their acts.
- may be inadequately dressed for the weather.
- may be emaciated or may have distended stomachs indicative of malnutrition. (See Appendix A for a quick reference chart of these indicators.)

Neglected adolescents tend to demonstrate many of these symptoms, but they may escape the well-intended intervention of educators by dropping out of school. They may also exhibit a pattern of early emancipation from their families with the promise of drifting into unfulfilled or even crime-ridden lives.

Neglected children of all ages are accustomed to a lifestyle devoid of routine and organization. They may demonstrate this in their own lives. For example, an inability to organize, or a lack of cleanliness and order is not unlikely. It is important to realize that many neglected children represent just one more generation characterized by their lifestyle. Their grandparents' teachers may also have been concerned with similar problems. Children learn parenting from their parents—they are their role models. Generation after generation of inadequate and neglectful role models, with no intervention, will create individuals who are only negatively prepared for parenting. Because of its pervasive nature, neglect is difficult to deal with. Where does the cycle end in the cases of parents with unmet needs who, in turn, are unable to meet the needs of their offspring? Only through intervention can this neglectful pattern be changed. Although children may be adequately fed and clothed, taught proper hygiene and given affection and attention, their parents too must be helped in order to break the cycle of neglect. This topic is discussed in Chapter 9.

Emotional Abuse

Emotional abuse refers to belittling, rejecting, and in general not providing a positive, loving, emotional atmosphere in which a child can grow.

This is perhaps the most difficult area to detect or prove and certainly difficult to report. Social service agencies are so overwhelmed with physical and sexual injuries that the less concrete report of emotional abuse may be screened out. That is, an agency may decide after reviewing the evidence that it is insufficient to warrant further investigation. This type of abuse is no less frustrating for the classroom teacher, however.

•

Tom, psychologically abused by his father, did not have the emotional strength necessary to learn to read in the first, second, or third grades. He just sat in school and relaxed in the warm, loving atmosphere. Outwardly cheerful and happy, his way of coping was to turn all negative incidents into jokes, but he manifested his problems by bizarre behavior such as eating (and swallowing) his shirts.

•

Indicators of emotional abuse, some of which Tom demonstrated, include the following:

• inappropriate affect such as turning negatives into jokes, or laughing when in pain
• extremes in behavior—overly happy or affectionate
• withdrawal—or no verbal or physical communication with others
• bizarre behavior such as self-destruction

- destructive behavior
- inordinate attention to details
- cruelty, vandalism, stealing, cheating
- rocking, thumbsucking, enuresis, or other habitual problems
- substance abuse (drugs or alcohol)
- anorexia nervosa (especially in adolescents)
- physical manifestations such as asthma, ulcers, or severe allergies
- delinquent behavior (especially in adolescents). (See Appendix A for a quick reference chart of these indicators.)

Emotionally abusive parents may have unrealistically high expectations of their offspring. When the children are unable to meet these expectations they receive verbal criticism that makes them feel incompetent and generally "bad." Such expectations may be related to some values or ideas the parent holds, as the following example illustrates:

•

Sally demonstrated her abuse by a perpetually sad expression. She looked as if she had just been beaten, but her father never touched her. Instead he berated her: "How did I ever deserve a girl? Girls are lesser beings." He had her hair cut in an unbecoming style, saying there was no point in trying to make an ugly girl look any better. He demanded complete obedience and subservience, including having her stand beside him as he ate to cut and salt his food. He rationalized this activity saying that her only hope in life was to be of use to a husband, if in fact anyone would want her. Even when Sally scored 160 on an IQ test, her father assured her the teachers were wrong—she was only a girl. Unfortunately she believed him.

•

Children suffering from emotional abuse may exhibit much the same behavior (in terms of acting out or exhibiting a poor self-image) as those suffering from physical abuse. In some cases, the emotionally neglected child may be generally ignored. In the J. family, for example, 16-year-old Tammie did not meet the family's standards of high intelligence. She was treated as if she did not exist, while her sisters and brothers received parental attention and concern.

Unfortunately, emotional abuse may not be easy to pinpoint. Many situations are not as clear-cut as those suggested here. Although most state statutes mention emotional abuse, it is difficult to prove. Teachers can help these child victims, however, with attention and encouragement to express themselves. (See Chapter 7 for specific suggestions.) In some cases the parents may merely need to know more about their child's need or they may need counseling to help them with their own problems.

CHAPTER 2

How to Recognize Sexual Abuse

•

Debbie, 14, had a "reputation" in school. She was not popular in the healthy sense of the word, she was talked about. Teachers observed her provocative behavior in their classes. According to rumors, she could be approached by any boy who sought a sexual experience. The tight-fitting clothes over her well-developed figure necessitated several visits to the assistant principal who tried to encourage more appropriate dress. School personnel assumed that her behavior was indicative of an inappropriately expressed sexual awakening colored by a poor self-image. When Debbie finally ran away from home, the story came out. She had been sexually abused by her father since the age of 9.

•

Sexual abuse has always been a human problem, but there has perhaps never been more awareness of it than at present. Social workers estimate that between 60 and 75 percent of the reported cases of child abuse are of sexual abuse. The Child Welfare League of America reported a 59 percent increase in child sexual abuse cases, from 35,014 in 1983 to 55,596 in 1984 (10). (See Appendix B, Tables 1, 2, and 3.) There is no way of knowing how many cases go unreported due to the taboo nature of this topic.

The question is repeatedly asked, "Is sexual abuse just more widely reported today or has it actually increased?" Although some theorists favor the high-report explanation, researcher Diana Russell (41) contends that both incest and extrafamilial abuse

Dear Camp Tallchief Staff,

At Camp Tallchief we use the timeless 'camp name' tradition, unique to Girl Scouts. It may seem an odd practice, but its base is more practical than ever. During staff training, you are being prepared for the awesome task of caretaker for our most precious resource. Our goal is to create an improved child-centered camp. As a camp counselor, you will need to call upon the best part of yourself and leave the rest behind. Each of you will take on a 'camp name' to help ease the campers and remind yourself why you are here.

No, Jane Doe with all her bills, meetings, classes, and phone messages does not work here. But 'Dune Buggy' the lifeguard, song leader, and trail guide does work here.

My camp name is Skipper. I love sailing, am a sailing instructor, and am the leader of this "ship." Some examples of camp names from previous staff are Buddha, Peaches, Reese, Rhinestone, and Smurfette.

Before you arrive at Camp Tallchief, you should put some serious thought into your camp name and have one picked out. Your camp name should instill confidence and have a positive nature. Be prepared to explain to the rest of the staff what your camp name is and the reason(s) why you have chosen it.

A parent may look at you funny when you tell them your name is 'Dune Buggy'. You will just explain to them that it's a camp name so the girls don't have to call you ma'am, and a reminder to staff that camp is all about the girl and her camp experience. Dune Buggy has no worries of her own that aren't concerned with camp. When the girls call your camp name, it reminds you where you are, why you are here, and whose needs are most important.

"Skipper"
Camp Director

have quadrupled from 1900 to 1973. She accounts for the increase by citing several changes in societal views and values. First, Russell blames the flourishing child pornography business as not only a stimulant for perpetrators but also as a means of engaging children in sexuality through their use as subjects in pornographic films and photographs. Second, the current sexual revolution permits a variety of sexual lifestyles. And the sexual equality movement results in some men being increasingly threatened by adult females and attracted to the pliable, cooperative, adoring faces of young girls used seductively to enhance TV ads. Russell also suggests that the lack of expertise in treating sexual abuse until recently has accounted for the numbers of perpetrators, who, abused as children, have gone on to repeat their victimization by abusing others. Finally, David Finkelhor (18) has demonstrated that the incidence of sexual abuse is higher among families with stepfathers. To absolve innocent stepparents, it should be noted that the abuse is not always at the hands of the new spouse; it may also result from two other factors. Statistically, children of a reconstituted family have been exposed to a greater number of men if their mother has dated before her remarriage. And the male friends of the stepfather may not perceive the same taboo in molesting the stepdaughter of their friend as they would in the case of his blood daughter. Whatever the reason given—the increased divorce rate or the current number of stepparent families—more children are vulnerable (41).

It becomes obvious, then, that sexual abuse is a major problem in society today. As in Debbie's case, the symptoms may be mistaken for other problems.

What is meant by sexual abuse? It refers to sexual involvement imposed upon a child by an adult who has greater "power, knowledge, and resources" (42, p. 78). Finkelhor points out the child's inability to consent, which, he says, is based upon knowledge and authority, neither of which is at the child's command (16).

•

Throughout her whole first grade year, six-year-old June had had at least six urinary tract infections, for which she was medicated periodically. Her teacher wondered if there were any tie between this problem and sexual abuse. The teacher knew that June's mother worked nights and that her new husband of 18 months babysat for June and her three-year-old brother.

It should be mentioned that aside from irritations from some forms of bubble bath and other rare, organic causes, it is not common for little girls to have the frequent urinary tract infections with which adult women may be plagued. The appearance of such recurrent infections would (at least) suggest the possibility of sexual abuse as the cause. As the story unfolded, it became evident that June was being sexually abused by her stepfather. Her teacher's report made it possible for the family to receive much needed help.

•

The most classic myth regarding sexual abuse is that it is perpetrated by strangers. Parents tell their children not to talk to strangers and not to take candy from strangers, for example. Certainly this is good parental advice. The fact remains, however, that between 70 and 85 percent of sexual abuse is committed by someone known—and often loved—by the child. Most perpetrators are male, although females are sometimes reported. The victims may be female or male, but females are more frequently seen in reports.

Children may be sexually abused at any age, but those who are prepubescent may be at more risk, due to their budding sexuality. Finkelhor (18) cites the period between ages 8 and 12 as the most vulnerable time, but much younger children have also been abused. By the time the abuse is uncovered, in most cases it has been continuing for between one and three years. According to Suzanne Sgroi, sexual abuse is characterized by a progression of sexual activity (44). It may begin with disrobing on the part of the perpetrator, or close observation of the child during bathing, dressing, or elimination rituals. Many sexual encounters begin with apparently innocent "horseplay" or kissing and progress to fondling, genital exposure, and mutual masturbation. Oral-genital contact, as well as anal contact, may follow, depending upon the opportunities available and the willingness of the child. Vaginal penetration with the fingers or penis often happens only after the perpetrator has carefully moved the child along to a level of readiness and trust. Experts are discovering, however, that even the first phases can create guilt and shame and can be almost as damaging as later phases (44, pp. 10–11).

Secrecy is a very important part of the whole picture in sexual abuse. While physical abuse may have its element of secrecy, society's horror of sexual deviation creates a need in the perpetrator to be especially careful in compelling quiet in the victim. Although threats or special attention may be enough to ensure some children's silence, sexual abusers may also use gifts, money, special outings, or edible treats. Charlotte Vale Allen in her account of her own sexual abuse speaks of finding change in her pockets after her father's abuse (2). Elements of this secrecy may be exhibited in a variety of ways. For example, the child may refuse to undress for gym, feeling that the teacher or peers can detect the sexual abuse just by seeing the unclothed body. It should be noted that failure to report sexual abuse can actually perpetuate the secrecy by aiding the perpetrator rather than the child.

Indicators of sexual abuse include—

- frequent urinary infections
- an inordinate number of gifts, or money from a questionable source
- exceptional secrecy
- more sexual knowledge than is appropriate for the child's age (especially in younger children)
- in-depth sexual play with peers (in younger children different from the normal "playing doctor" form of exploration)

- overcompliance or withdrawal
- overaggressiveness, acting out
- sexually provocative or promiscuous behavior (in adolescents) or otherwise acting out sexually
- an inordinate fear of males or seductiveness toward males
- a drop in school performance or sudden nonparticipation in school activities
- sleep problems such as nightmares or insomnia
- crying without provocation
- rashes or itching in genital areas, scratching the area a great deal or figeting when seated
- sudden onset of enuresis (wetting pants or bed) or soiling
- sudden phobic behavior
- symptoms associated with venereal disease, such as—vaginal pain, vaginal or penile discharge (in young children), genital or oral sores, frequent sore throats (may indicate gonococcal infection of the pharynx or throat)
- diagnosis of genital warts
- feelings of little self-worth, talk of being "damaged"
- pain in the genital area (which may be from lacerations)
- excessive bathing
- frequent vomiting
- excessive masturbation
- appearing much older and more worldly than peers
- great anxiety
- suicide attempts (especially among adolescents)
- runaway from home, excessively (especially adolescents)
- early pregnancies (in adolescents). (See Appendix A for a quick reference chart of these indicators.)

It is easier to deny the symptoms of sexual abuse than it is to overlook physical abuse or neglect. It is also not quite so difficult to imagine that a prominent member of the community has "disciplined a child a little too severely"—perhaps because of stress—as it is to entertain the idea that he has been sexually involved with his daughter.

For sexual abuse to occur, several contributing factors are necessary. The first is *opportunity*. Often there is the profile of a mother who works in the evening or at other times when a child may be most vulnerable. Or a mother may not be otherwise available—during times of illness, depression, or involvement outside the home, for example. Many sources also caution against the teenage male babysitter who is not involved with his peers and who does not have a strong male figure with whom to identify.

Another contributing factor to sexual abuse is *change*. Families have frequently undergone some recent stress such as relocation, unemployment, newly employed mother, or illness, which makes the members vulnerable. Many families may be candidates for either sexual or physical abuse due to frequent moves. Also present in many sexual abuse situations is trust. More often than not, perpetrators occupy or assume a position that the child trusts, which makes their actions possible.

Some attention should be given to "stranger danger," the assault (usually one-time) of a child by a stranger. Although the family may not appear to be directly involved in such cases, it is vital that family members, too, receive help and possibly treatment. The trauma of child molestation is devastating to some families; the parents' reaction may well determine the child's ability to handle the memory in later life (44, p. 111).

The degree of trauma experienced by a sexually abused child depends upon the following factors:

1. *The identity of the perpetrator*. Betrayal of trust is an important aspect of abuse. The

closer the bond of trust between victim and perpetrator, the more likely the trauma.

2. *The duration of the abuse*. Abuse that continues over a longer period of time has the potential for being more emotionally assaultive and therefore more traumatic than abuse that occurs over a shorter period.

3. *The extent of the abuse*. The child who is fondled while clothed may experience less guilt and subsequent trauma than the child who is exposed to rectal or vaginal intercourse. Physical harm may also serve to intensify trauma.

4. *The age of the child*. This factor may influence how well the abuse is integrated. Each age has its developmental task. Regression or the inability to master a particular task may indicate the age at which the abuse occurred. At some ages, abuse presents more roadblocks for children than at others.

5. *The first reactions of significant people*. Some therapists feel that the reception of the child's story by others can influence the degree of trauma experienced. Disbelief or overreaction at the time of disclosure intensifies the child's feelings of guilt and blame. For this reason, teachers must understand sexual abuse in order to support a child's disclosure calmly and competently.

6. *The point at which and the way in which the abuse is disclosed*. Some abuse is disclosed accidentally. The teacher recognizes symptoms or the child's classmate reports suspicious sexual behavior. But some children disclose the abuse themselves. In these instances, there is usually a reason. For example, a child may have just realized that the abuse was wrong; an older child may be unable to interact with peers and may feel that disclosure of the abuse will relieve this pressure. Some victims perceive that their younger siblings are vulnerable to the perpetrator and disclose in order to protect them. Another important reason—children may feel they will be believed. A sympathetic teacher whom they have learned to trust may be the person with whom

they feel comfortable enough to unburden themselves of their secret.

      *7. The personality structure of the vic-
tim.* This factor also influences the amount of trauma
resulting from the abuse. Two abused children in the
same family, for example, may react totally differently. Learning about the personality style of a particular child in their classroom who they feel has been
victimized may help teachers recognize how this
child will react and how to minimize the resultant
trauma (46).

      Although it is usually assumed that
girls are the victims of sexual abuse and its trauma,
boys are also vulnerable, as described in the following section.

Boys as Forgotten Victims of Child Sexual Abuse

      Recently the literature has been re-
minding us that boys too are victims of child sexual
abuse as well as of physical abuse and neglect. Yet,
for several reasons, we tend to forget that boys are
as vulnerable as their female counterparts. First, in
our culture, it is difficult to see males as victims.
The female is the perennial victim. According to the
conscious or unconscious argument, the male should
be able to protect himself or run. Second, boys have
learned that admitting to being victimized subjects
them to being seen as "sissies," which often invites
teasing or more abuse from peers who see them as
vulnerable. Third, society has a double standard.
While girls are theoretically to be protected from
sexual relations before adulthood and marriage, there
is an often unexpressed feeling that early sexuality
for boys is almost a rite and therefore expected.
Take, for example, *The Summer of '42.* Nowhere did
that movie indicate that the seduction of a young boy
by an older woman was to be considered abuse. It is
assumed that boys *want* the sexual experience, how-

ever coercive it might be. For this reason many boys do not report such occurrences as negative. Finkelhor estimates that approximately 2.5 to 5 percent of boys under the age of 13 have had sexual experiences with adults. This may not seem like a high percentage. However, of the 22 million boys under 13 in the United States today, a total of 550,000 to 1,100,000 will eventually be victimized (18, p. 155).

Why don't boys talk more about being abused? The answer may lie partially in the reasons given for the difficulties associated with seeing boys as victims. Boys grow up with a "male ethic of self-reliance"; talking about victimization labels them. But the reasons go beyond these factors. Males appear to be much more concerned about the stigma of homosexuality. Since a high percentage of boys are abused by adult men (18), the fear is intensified. The abused boy fears being labeled homosexual and therefore will not tell others. His fear often makes him unwilling to face the victimization in his own mind.

●

A client in therapy was concerned about her nine-year-old son. Shawn had been behaving strangely—he was very moody and uncooperative; he was bossy with his younger sister, almost to the point of abuse. He had also developed an interest in guns and war toys—playthings that his parents did not encourage. His mother described him as "suddenly tough—a professional macho" in his behavior. After seeing Shawn for several therapy sessions, I began to suspect sexual abuse and asked him about it. The boy began to cry uncontrollably but finally was able to tell me about being sodomized by the adult brother of a friend. The brother had continued to abuse Shawn, suggesting that he tell no one lest people think Shawn was homosexual. So concerned was the boy that he had adopted his pseudomacho manner.

●

Another factor prevents boys from telling of their abuse. In our culture boys are given much more freedom in everyday life than girls. Male children are less closely supervised and are allowed to be without adult supervision much earlier than girls. Most parents who learned of a son's victimization outside the home would try to protect him from future occurrences. This protection would mean curtailing his activities, perhaps, but certainly more supervision. Thus the boy perceives that he would lose more than he would gain (18).

Boys also tend to be victimized at a much younger age than girls. Finkelhor postulates that girls are abused at a median age of about 12½, while boys are abused at a median age of about 8½. Only 26 percent of abused boys are over 13 as compared with 47 percent of abused girls. Younger children, too, are often less cognizant of the resources available to help them (18).

Boys are sometimes abused within the family in conjunction with their sisters. When female siblings are involved and a report is made, the victimization of the girl is often reported rather than that of the boy.

Finally, while the abuse of girls tends to come to the attention of child protection agencies, the abuse of boys is more likely to be reported to the police. Police involvement can be much more frightening for a young child than intervention by a plainclothes social worker. Thus boys may not want to report at all if they recognize from the experience of friends that the police will be called.

It is important for educators to be alert to the signals boys give that they have been victimized. Intervening in a nonthreatening manner can save a boy from growing up with the scars of his abuse. Since many perpetrators have a history of victimization in their childhoods, teachers may also be protecting future generations by breaking the cycle *now*.

Although they have come to understand the sexual assault of children and adolescents by adults, teachers must now recognize a new phenomenon that has gained increased attention—abuse by peers.

Acquaintance Rape

Sexual assault by an adult male or female is not necessarily the only concern of adolescents. Adults who guide adolescents are becoming increasingly aware of a phenomenon that is often called "acquaintance rape." For adolescents, this term refers to a sexual assault by a peer. It is not an old phenomenon. Women looking back on their teen years remember the subtle and sometimes not-too-subtle messages of their male peers that sex was required in order to continue dating. Other women recount being forced into having sexual intercourse because "she led him on" or "she owed him that after all the money he had spent." Boys are not thought of as being physically forced into sexual relations, but they are certainly vulnerable to being cajoled into having intercourse by a variety of verbal blackmail statements. *Nobody Told Me It Was Rape* (1) contains the results of an interesting survey. The study asked teens when it was "okay for a boy to hold a girl down and force her to have sexual intercourse." Respondents were asked to consider if rape were justified in several instances. The percentages of males and females who answered no were recorded. These students felt it was *NOT* okay in these instances (1, p.14):

	Percent Answering No	
	F	M
He spent a lot of money on her.	88%	61%
He is so turned on he can't stop.	79%	64%
She has had intercourse with other boys.	82%	61%
She is stoned or drunk.	82%	61%
She lets him touch her above the waist.	72%	61%
She says she's going to have sex with him, then changes her mind.	69%	46%
They have dated a long time.	68%	57%
She has led him on.	73%	46%
She gets him sexually excited.	58%	49%

Granted, the percentages of teens who do not feel these circumstances justify rape are high; they are not, however, very high. Consider the last two categories. Fifty four percent of the boys who perceived that a girl had "led him on" felt that rape was justified. Fifty one percent of the boys and 42 percent of the girls felt rape was justified if a girl was perceived to have gotten the boy so excited that he couldn't stop. Adams and Fay further discovered that *only* 34 percent of the teens felt rape was not justified in any of these situations.

Acquaintance rape among teens may not be unrelated to previous sexual abuse. Adolescents who have been sexually, physically, or emotionally abused are more likely to sexually assault peers (1). In addition, individuals who have been abused as children are more vulnerable to future abuse, especially in the teen years (41). Finally, adolescents with low self-esteem, for whatever reason, are more vulnerable to rape.

It is important, therefore, that teachers be involved in the prevention of date rape as well as of child abuse. But how? Adams and Fay (1, pp. 5–6) have suggested some guidelines for parents that I have adapted for teachers.

1. Decide what you consider to be rape. Do you feel rape is justified in any of the areas suggested in the Adams and Fay survey? In fact—*no one* has the right to force sexual activity on another for any reason.

2. Consider before the subject comes up, how you will feel about talking about rape with teens. Adolescents perceive adult discomfort and will often refuse to talk if they know adults are uncomfortable.

Consider stressing your concern about them rather than using scare tactics.

3. Consider also at what point the discussion will best fit in. The topic of acquaintance rape would lend itself to inclusion in a discussion of individual rights and personal choices. One could also consider the effect of the media on our lives, suggesting that the degree of sexuality in the media today may encourage acquaintance rape. (For example, jeans are sold by ads of overdeveloped teens who are draped, suggestively, across the television screen. The media implies that "macho" is in and that to be macho means to be tough. The implication in some ads is that women are weak and want to be treated accordingly.)

Or, a discussion of acquaintance rape may fit well into a human sexuality-biology or adolescent issues segment.

4. Be prepared for questions, discussion, and even to make referrals. Teens often have concerns about the urges they feel as a result of their developing sexual awareness. They may be wishing someone would talk with them about these concerns. Adolescents who have been raped may see your openness as an indication that they can confide in you. Local rape crisis centers, school counselors, local counseling agencies, or hotlines can suggest referrals.

Be conscious of the fact that date rape is not necessarily an indicator of the rapist's severe pathology. Granted, acquaintance rape can result from acting out prior victimization; it is also a product of our society. Adolescents today are trying to form values in an era of confused morals, an era in which they are encouraged to watch Rambo-like characters on the one hand and to hear the outcries against governments that do not respect the rights of their citizens on the other. These half children-half adults are also exploring their own sexuality at a time when society's views about sexuality are conflicting. The teacher's role is to open the channels of communication to enable adolescents to undertake that exploration with guidance. Sometimes to keep these channels open, teachers need to understand their own feelings and attitudes.

46

Understanding Ourselves

Given the high statistics of those who were abused or neglected as children (22, 48), it is quite possible that some teachers may have experienced maltreatment in their own childhood. Individuals have a variety of reactions to an abusive past at different points in their lives. Some survivors may want to search for answers, working out the hurt and anger they feel through understanding. Other past victims want to forget the subject completely. As I mentioned in the Introduction, information is everyone's best ally. For those whose past is preventing them from dispersing that information to others, there may be help. Remember the teacher mentioned in the Introduction who had been sexually abused and who wanted to be part of prevention efforts to protect her own children. Think of how much better the situation would have been for other adult victims if they had learned they could tell someone—or if the person they told was knowledgeable enough to believe them. Knowing that they will help to protect other children may encourage teachers who suffered abuse as children to become involved in prevention efforts. It may not, however, prevent them from being disturbed by the material on abuse as it reactivates old memories. If this is the case, perhaps it is time to seek help. More and more therapists are becoming skilled in talking with survivors of abusive homes—particularly sexually abusive homes. Therapy might also help those who were sexually abused outside the home. Those who cannot find a therapist who is knowledgeable about abuse should try one who treats adult children of alcoholics. The families of alcoholics and of abusers cope with similar issues. Numerous agencies conduct groups for adults who were sexually abused as children or who come from violent homes.

To find these therapists or groups in your community, call an agency dealing with child abuse (for example, the Department of Social Service, Child Protective Services) and ask for a referral for adult survivors. Rape crisis centers may also offer suggestions. Parents United or Parents Anonymous (see Appendix E for addresses) may be able to suggest groups for past victims of sexual abuse.

Teachers who are adult survivors of abuse owe it to themselves as well as to the children in their classroom to understand their own experiences.

To fully understand sexual abuse, all teachers must recognize the symptoms and causes, as well as their own feelings on the subject. It is also important to remember that sexual abuse—like physical abuse and neglect—is a family problem: for the child to receive the most effective help, family involvement is necessary. To give the family the best chance, early reporting and intervention are vital.

CHAPTER 3

The Reporting Process

Chapters 1 and 2 discussed many of the clues to look for in detecting child abuse. Once teachers are satisfied that they have indeed recognized such clues, it is necessary that they report suspected cases of abuse. First, however, there are three kinds of knowledge with which well-prepared educators should be armed even *before* encountering a case of child maltreatment. They are as follows:

1. Knowledge of the reporting laws of the state in which they teach

2. Knowledge of the school reporting policy or procedure, if one is available—for example, an outline of the steps to follow within the school or information on when a report should be made

3. Knowledge of or a relationship with (either through the school or personally) the protective agency designated to accept reports.

This chapter discusses these three kinds of knowledge.

State Reporting Laws

What is the legal role of the teacher in reporting the abuse and neglect of children? All states expect educators to be involved in reporting; many states back up this expectation with a fine (which in some cases may be up to $1,000) or a jail sentence for failure to report. The teacher is frequently referred to as a *mandated reporter*—that is, one who in his or her professional capacity is legally responsible for reporting to the local protective agency. In addition to educators, state statutes desig-

49

nate other mandatory reporters, including other school personnel, and the extent of their responsibility. (See Appendix C for a list of reporters.) Every school system, if not every teacher, should have a copy of the state regulations concerning reporting. They can usually be obtained through the local protective agency. Many agencies also publish interpretations of the statutes that are much easier to read and understand than the laws themselves. Appendix E contains a list of national organizations concerned with child abuse and neglect, including two national resource centers and a clearinghouse on child abuse and neglect information.

Liability is another issue that concerns educators. As mentioned earlier, there may be a fine or a jail sentence for *not* reporting. All states provide immunity for any professional who reports. (See Appendix F.) Various states protect the mandated reporter who reports "in good faith" or who has "reasonable cause to suspect abuse" (8, pp. 4–7). It is highly unlikely that an educator would be sued for reporting. Even if this did happen, the teacher who reported in good faith would not be found liable.

Whatever your state's stand on immunity, it is better legally and morally to report than not to report. Certainly it is wiser to make the local agency aware of a situation than to wait and perhaps subject a child to the risk of permanent harm or possible death.

School Reporting Policy

Although anyone associated with the school system is responsible for reporting, it is important that the system have, or at least begin to set up, a procedure for reporting. Such a policy should include specific information such as—

1. At what point should the teacher report child abuse? Suspicion? Reasonable cause to believe? (This may be based not only on school policy but also on state law.)

2. Whom does the teacher notify? Nurse? Principal? School social worker?
3. What specific information does the teacher need to know to report?
4. What actions should the teacher have taken before reporting to validate suspicions?
5. What other school personnel should be involved?
6. Who makes the report to the appropriate authorities? How?
7. What information should be included in the report? (This may be dictated by state law and protective agency policy.)
8. What followup is expected on reported cases?
9. What role will the school play in possible community/child protection teams?
10. What commitment does the school have to in-service training or community programs?

The existence of such a policy and knowledge of it in advance will be extremely helpful to teachers. Immediately after you have discovered huge bruises on the arms of a student is not the opportune time to try to discover to whom you should report. But if the school does not have a policy, certainly the principal should be made aware of the situation. If you are convinced that a case should be reported, either you, the principal, the school nurse, or the school social worker or counselor would be the most likely person to report. Remember, however, that notifying a superior of your suspicions does not make you personally less liable.

Teachers frequently ask, "What if I report an abusive situation to an administrator who does not feel it should be reported or who feels that there is something wrong with me that I cannot handle the problem myself?" The school administration *should* be involved. A child abuse report is, in effect, based upon the decision of the educational team serving the child. As noted previously, many states consider every school professional a mandated reporter who is therefore responsible. In some cases, administrators may not be familiar with the magnitude of their responsibility in this area or they may feel that reporting will be a reflection upon their school. In fact, reporting a family distress situation points to a school system that is knowledgeable about potential barriers to student learning and concerned about overcoming them. If, however, your administrator will not report and refuses to let you do so, you must make a choice—to try harder to convince the administrator of the severity of the situation, to try to obtain permission to report from the administrator's superior, or to report the situation yourself. (Some states allow anonymous reporting.) Certainly neither of the last two courses of action should be taken without a great deal of thought. But whether the administrator agrees to report or not, two factors still exist: (1) you are legally liable until a report is made, and (2) the child may be in danger. The following was recounted by an extremely distraught and guilt-ridden teacher:

●

I knew Henry was being beaten by his mother. My colleagues knew it too, and each one had approached our principal individually. Finally, after Henry received a particularly bad beating, I pleaded with the principal to allow me to report. When he flatly refused, I felt I had no recourse. Several days later Henry did not come to school. When I arrived home, my husband greeted me with the evening paper. Henry was dead—a victim of child abuse.

●

The decision not to report child abuse is not a callous or vindictive one; often it is merely a mistake of judgment. Knowing the consequences of not reporting, as well as the procedures for reporting, should make the decision much easier.

One solution to the seemingly overwhelming responsibility of reporting is to have the school policy designate a school team (composed of the school counselor or social worker, nurse, administrator, and teachers, for example) to discuss the potential report and later to provide mutual help in the justification and followup of the report. This method relieves any one teacher of pressure and also offers peer support.

Protective Agencies

Reporting to the designated protective agency (most often the state or county welfare agency) usually means a telephone call to give the agency the information necessary to begin an investigation. (See Appendix D.) State law usually requires the following information:

- names of the child and parents
- address
- age and sex of the child
- type and extent of the child's injuries or complaints
- evidence of prior injuries
- explanation of the injuries given by the child
- name and telephone number of the reporter
- actions taken by the reporter (such as detaining the child, photographs)
- other pertinent information.

To this point it has been assumed that the teacher uncovers the abuse. If, however, the child reports to the teacher, it is important to listen in a way that demonstrates your care and concern. Obtain as many facts and details as possible without appearing to conduct an interrogation. Some children may try to swear you to secrecy, yet the fact that they have confided in you is a cry for help. Tell the child sensitively that you must report the situation and why, and do so at the time. For example, you might say, "Daddy needs help. It's not good for him to be doing this to you. I'm afraid you'll get hurt again, and I care about you." Such an explanation is an assurance of your concern not only for the child's welfare, but also for the parent's welfare.

Then, it is important to persuade the child to remain at school while you report the case. If the child goes home immediately after telling you about the situation, there may be several negative results:

1. The child may feel guilty to the point of refuting

the story when questioned later. (This is especially likely in cases of sexual abuse.)

2. The child may be subject to further abuse when the parent discovers the disclosure.

3. The child may be fearful of facing the parent and run away from home, resulting eventually in more abuse.

Teachers can usually keep younger children interested in the classroom, giving themselves time to report. If you explain the situation sensitively and carefully to older children, they may agree to wait in the classroom. Needless to say, you should know the exact reporting procedure. You should also tell the agency that the child is at school and urge an immediate response. A note of caution for the concerned teacher: Do not take the child to your own home. Such an act of benevolence may seem to provide the temporary protection the child needs, but it may place you in legal jeopardy. If your state does not give you the legal right to detain a child, you may even be charged with kidnapping. It is better to work within the social service system than to put yourself in a legally precarious position.

If the child refuses to wait, tell the agency and urge immediate action. Social service personnel usually consider such situations to be emergencies so that the agency should be able to act at once. In the meantime, it is important to explain carefully to the child exactly what is happening.

Whether the case is an emergency or not, many states require that a written report follow the oral report within 24 to 72 hours. The school should have the appropriate forms for the written followup. (See Appendix H for a filled-in sample.) This form is sent to the agency designated to receive reports. It may be vital that the agency have this written notification as well as the telephone call in order to begin a thorough investigation. Reporters should keep a copy of any report they submit for their own and/or the school's records. Of course the information should be kept confidential.

One of the best ways to obtain results on an abuse report is to use documented material—written descriptions of bruises, dates, the accounts of several people, and any other data may be helpful. Legally teachers should not undress a child to discover bruises, but school nurses may have this prerogative. Some school systems have photographed children's bruises. The legality of this practice in a particular state should be carefully checked with the local social service agency. (Also see Appendix F.) Talking with a social worker may also help teachers determine the viability of their reports.

Once the agency receives the report, it determines if there is sufficient evidence to warrant an investigation or, in the case of an emergency, immediate action. This decision or screening process may be completed instantly, or it may take a day or even a week, depending on the emergency nature of the case. A decision to screen in the case means that a social worker or team of social workers will investigate it. Here again, the nature of the case determines how soon action will be taken. Most states mandate an investigation within a week or two, or sooner in an emergency—such as when a child's health is severely threatened or when a delay would cause some immediate danger to the child.

When calling in a report, you may want to ask about the timetable of the agency. You can also assure the social worker of your continued cooperation and ask to be kept informed of the progress of the case. In some states social workers cannot divulge the results of an investigation without the signed affidavit of the alleged abuser, but they may be able to assure you that the case is being investigated. Also, even though some social workers may not keep a reporter informed, many do—especially if they feel that the teacher can continue to be a resource in helping the child and the family.

The important thing to remember at this point is that your report sets in motion the helping process that the family so desperately needs.

Teachers sometimes complain that they have made an abuse report and they feel that the social service agency has "done nothing." First, it is important to realize that the social service agency operates under a legal mandate from the state or county. This legal framework often requires that social workers provide certain facts to justify validation of abuse. If those facts are not available, the case may be "screened out" (i.e., the agency cannot act without further information). As a teacher in contact with the child daily, your documentation may help the social worker intervene. If a case *is* screened out and you are then able to document evidence of further abuse, do not be afraid to file another report or encourage a colleague who may also be close to the situation to file.

If you do not understand what is happening in a case and are unable to reach the social worker involved, contact the supervisor. Like teachers who find it easier to respond to a concerned parent than to a critical one, social workers and supervisors will be more likely to answer questions when they perceive that the teacher is expressing concern, rather than suggesting incompetence. Perhaps the best way to ensure communication with the social service agency is through personal contact. Set up the previously mentioned child protection team with at least one agency worker or supervisor as a member. Or request that a social worker or supervisor serve as a liaison with the school. If your school is not receptive to these suggestions, call the local social service agency yourself. Say that you are a concerned teacher and would like to talk about your role in the reporting process with a social worker or supervisor.

Remember that the helping team needs to present a *united* front as a model for the child who may already be suffering from the confusion brought about by a disorganized, abusive, or neglectful family.

CHAPTER 4

How to Validate Suspicion of Child Abuse

As indicated in Chapter 3, each state has its own set of reporting regulations, which may differ considerably from each other. Some states require teachers to report immediately even in cases of suspected abuse or neglect. Other states allow more leeway and expect that cases will be fairly well documented when reported. This chapter offers suggestions to help teachers validate their suspicions of child abuse and thus improve the reporting process. If your state says, "Report even if you only suspect," your sensitivity to validation will enable you to help the social service system either to create a more pressing reason for opening the case, to build a stronger case for court, or to provide additional information to help the social worker work out the best treatment plan. If, on the other hand, your state requires proof of your suspicions, the suggestions provided here will help you supply the proof.

Documentation

It is important to have as much information as possible about a situation when reporting. Documentation greatly helps. For example, every time a student comes to class with bruises, jot down the date, the type of bruises, and the child's explanation for them. Also note any contacts you may have had with parents, including their reactions to you as well as their interaction with the child. When you report, or at the time of later court intervention, such documented, factual information will be extremely valuable.

One way to discover more facts about the home situation and to involve parents initially is to treat whatever problem the child exhibits as one that requires special assessment. Through Public Law 94-142, the teacher can request a care evaluation. This consists of a series of tests and assessments focusing on educational needs and describing what the child can or cannot do. It usually culminates in a conference of parents and the professionals concerned with the evaluation. Since the child may also be exhibiting learning difficulties, such an evaluation can be easily justified. Some abuse cases have been handled voluntarily in this way without any court intervention.

Analyzing Data

The next step is to analyze your data. For example, for the child who frequently comes to class with bruises, is there anything else about the child's behavior that fits the physical or behavioral clues given in Chapter 1? Have you observed the child and parents together? Do the parents' expectations for the child appear to be too high for a child of that age?

One teacher invites all parents, with their children, for a visit during the school year. At this time she asks each child to demonstrate a task (usually one necessitating adult help), and then she observes any interaction between parent and child. She finds that the interaction gives her invaluable information. As an example, she cites her interview with Danny and his mother.

●

Mrs. K. greeted me as follows: "I'm not surprised that you have asked me to come in. Now *you* know that Danny is nothing like his older brother, Ed. Ed was so good in school and so cooperative. Then there's Danny!" She indicated the 11-year-old boy standing sullenly behind her. I asked Mrs. K. to sit down and suggested that Danny hang their coats in the back of the room while I got some notes.

"For goodness sakes, Danny! Don't drag my coat," Mrs. K. admonished. "And hang it up right."

Danny did not respond but continued to complete his task. "Stand up straight, Daniel," Mrs. K. barked. "It's so tough with these kids," she remarked to me. "Being a mother *and* father is no picnic! In fact, will we be long? I have to pick up my son Ed at a friend's house. Danny, come over here and sit down."

Danny was quietly observing the fish in their tank— moving in endless circles with no hope of escape in their monotonous search for variety in the confines of the tank. Suddenly I saw Danny's life much like that.

Mrs. K.'s further comments made it quite clear to me that no matter what Danny did, he could never meet her expectations. Was the abuse we had observed a symbol of her own frustrations?

●

Not every teacher has an opportunity to observe either parent or student so closely. At the high school level, a teacher may see the adolescent only for brief class periods. As one instructor noted, "My geometry class is not exactly the arena for sharing feelings. How do *I* know if a child is being abused?" In such situations, teachers need to be observant—that is, aware of peculiar behavior or unusual appearance on the part of the student. Further, they can demonstrate an attitude of openness. A chemistry teacher, for example, in spite of her no-nonsense facts and figures in class, inspired students to come to her after class because of her open, accepting attitude. Although high school teachers who do not have home room or advisory responsibilities may not be in a position to report because of lack of information, through observation they may be able to provide valuable support to colleagues who do report.

Consulting Other Professionals

It is important for teachers who suspect abuse or neglect to explore the interactions of their colleagues with the child. Talk with other teachers. Have they noticed these bruises or this behavior? The physical education teacher or the coach, for example, may have noticed bruises as the child changed clothes for gym. If so, you have additional support. It is also important to consult and work with other professionals within the school system. School nurses have the medical expertise to examine bruises, burns, and untreated medical problems. They may be the only ones who have the right to remove a child's clothing; they may also have the right to take photographs of any bruises they uncover. In addition, nurses are in an excellent position to teach the neglected child some basic rules of personal hygiene.

School psychologists are trained not only in testing, which can be helpful in detecting children's problems, but they are also schooled in human motivation and, possibly, counseling. They may not only help the child through diagnosis and counseling, but may be of help to you as a consultant. School social workers, also trained in counseling, are frequently the professionals most likely to act as links between the child's family and the school, perhaps even making home visits. Valuable information can be gathered from observing the family's attitude toward the child. Are the parents responsive to school intervention? Do they want to help the child or do they see the child as an unwelcome responsibility?

Special education teachers also see a large percentage of child abuse victims. According to a study by James Christiansen, the spelling, math, and reading scores as well as the overall academic achievement of abused children were significantly lower than those of children not subjected to abuse

(11). In addition, victims of maltreatment exhibited more psychological and behavioral problems that brought them to the attention of the special education teacher.

Depending upon their size, some schools may or may not have these professionals available, or their duties may be assumed by others. Any careful observer can, in fact, be of help in detecting problems of abuse. In one school, for example, a librarian who has great sensitivity to children and their needs uncovers more cases of maltreatment than any other faculty member. Whatever the school situation, as you attempt to validate your suspicions that a child has been physically abused, neglected, or sexually abused, remember that these colleagues can be of assistance.

In addition to professionals within the school, community agencies that work with abused children can be helpful. Agency representatives can be invited to speak to faculty members about their responsibilities in the reporting procedure. Or individual teachers can make contact with a social worker or supervisor whom they can call to discuss suspicions they may have but do not feel comfortable about reporting. (As a former social worker, I would have much preferred to discuss a case with a teacher than to receive an unsubstantiated report that would later be thrown out, to the frustration of all concerned parties.)

Alternative Steps

A frequent problem for many teachers is student hygiene. For example, a student may come to school very poorly dressed, unkempt, dirty, eliciting complaints from other children about body odor. It is easy to assume that this is a case of blatant neglect. If a child neglect report is filed, however, it may well be screened out when it is discovered that an otherwise loving parent has similar habits of personal hygiene.

This type of situation can provide an example of alternative steps to take before reporting. Poor hygiene is not an uncommon problem, and for the most part it is not life-threatening. You can consult the school nurse and perhaps call the parent in to discuss the case, discreetly and in a nonthreatening, informal way. Sometimes a well-meaning parent who discovers that a child is having difficulty with peers due to an odor problem will gladly attempt to remedy the situation. Or you may uncover concerns about housing, sanitation, or financial need for which the parent can be referred to the appropriate agency.

If, however, after talking with the parent, there appears to be neglect, you will feel more secure about reporting the situation.

Communicating with the Child

As you attempt to validate your concerns about abuse or neglect, your immediate response may be to talk with the child. This may not be advisable for several reasons:

1. The child may be afraid to tell the truth because of—

   • fear of being hurt by the abuser

   • belief that "people go to jail for abuse" (admittedly in some states a jail sentence is a reality, but it is hoped that the child can be helped by a social worker or counselor to deal with this reality)

   • fear that something will happen to him/her (such as removal from the home)

   • loyalty to the parent—no matter how bad the situation may be.

2. The child may feel that the abuse is deserved.

3. While some children may be relieved by the

outlet of talking to a sympathetic adult, others may be threatened and withdraw from you.

4. Neglected children may know nothing but neglect.

The best approach is to assure children that you can be approached when they are ready to talk. If a child wants to talk or comes to you to report, listen sensitively, being concerned not only with the youngster's feelings, needs, and comfort, but also with accumulating the data necessary for reporting. Puppet shows, movies, and filmstrips such as *Sometimes It's Okay to Tattle* are useful to show in the classroom. (See Appendix I.) They may elicit reports from children by helping them realize that there is a problem and it is all right to talk about it. For sexual abuse, discussions about the body and each person's right not to be touched without permission can be helpful.

Another method that may inspire a report—especially from young children—is the use of art or play techniques. A classic technique is to ask all the children to draw pictures of themselves and their families. Much can be learned from the activities shown and, in particular, the child's position in the picture. Children frequently speak and draw in metaphors. For example, the physically abused child is often a scapegoat, singled out from siblings. Thus, you may notice that youngsters you suspect of being abused draw pictures depicting themselves as being different or removed in some way from other members of their families. Sexually abused children may be more precise anatomically than other children of their age group. Both sexually abused girls and boys may also draw structures that resemble sexual organs or they may concentrate on intrusive themes (38, 44, 45). Neglected children may have trouble organizing their thoughts or they may use depressed scenes or colors. Since most teachers are not specifically trained in interpreting children's art work, you may wish to consult the school psychologist for an analysis of the content of such drawings. These details are mentioned here to sensitize concerned teachers to material that may be looked at in greater depth.

Although drawing is most frequently associated with younger children, it can be employed with older children in a more symbolic way. For example, "Create a scrapbook or book of drawings about your future. Describe all aspects of your life— your future family, your career, etc." Such an assignment may well uncover the theme "I don't want to do to my kids what my parents did to me!" Older students can also be encouraged to read a book about a family and write a report comparing it to their own.

The validation process may require a few hours or a few weeks, depending upon the potential threat to the child. Neglect and sexual abuse, while potentially destructive, have been continuing for some time. It is better to have clear-cut facts than to report and have the case screened out because of insufficient evidence. Physical abuse, on the other hand, may be life-threatening. Therefore, teachers should report suspected physical abuse as soon as possible. Even in these cases, however, the more factual information you can provide, the more likely it is that something will be done for the child once you have reported.

Communicating with the Parents

If you have concluded that the child is in fact abused or neglected, at what point should you inform the parents? Your first inclination may be to inform the parents that you intend to report. Such an action may pose several problems, however. Consider what may happen in some cases of maltreatment. In neglectful situations the lifestyle may be chaotic and the roots few. A neglectful parent who feels threatened may flee. The same may be true in abuse situations. Mary Jane Chalmers wrote an account of an abusive and neglectful family whose itinerant career prevented detection until it was too late (9).

In addition to flight, there is also the possibility that knowledge of the report may increase the danger to the child, especially if the child is the reporter. Abuse is associated with control—the parent feels desperately out of control and strikes out. The introduction of the social service system or the legal system into the family's life creates an even more vulnerable situation. If the parent feels this threat, the child may in fact suffer more abuse.

Other phenomena operate in cases of sexual abuse. For both victim and perpetrator (especially in cases of incest), there is a higher risk of suicide immediately after a report is made. Once the situation comes to light, the case *must* be handled swiftly and with expert timing.

Certainly the parents must know that the abuse or neglect has been or is to be reported. Social workers differ in their advice as to when to inform the parents, however. Considering the possible parental reactions mentioned, some feel that teachers should report before informing the parents, but that the parents should subsequently be approached by those who are specifically trained to deal with them. Knowledge of such support should be reassuring to teachers.

Other social workers feel that the parents are owed an explanation before the report is made for the following reasons:

1. The situation may be a misunderstanding and once all the parties communicate, a report may be deemed unnecessary.

2. Parents may feel less threatened, more amenable to cooperation and therefore more willing to seek help if they are approached before the involvement of the social service system. Considering that control is a central issue, especially for abusive parents, it is important to deprive them of as little control as possible.

Because of this difference of opinion among social service personnel concerning parental rights, cooperation, and the child's safety, teachers may want to consult social workers informally for advice.

In some cases, once the report has been made, you may have an opportunity to talk with the child or the parent about the report. But by this time you should have the support of other professionals. Whether or not you see the parent may depend largely on your role in the school and your desire, if any, to further your involvement.

Reporting a child abuse case is not easy for teachers emotionally. Many, although desiring to help the child, feel unsure of their own position and also of the effect the report will have on their future relationship with both child and parents. Some teachers fear repercussions from the family. Physically, the abusive family is dangerous to the child but not usually to adults. Some families may try to "fight back" legally, but teachers who have acted in good faith are legally safe. The worst fear of many educators is that the family may strike out emotionally by making threats to them or false statements to others. However, anyone can be a victim of this type of behavior—from a vindictive neighbor or from a family reported for abuse. The support of colleagues can enable teachers to better handle such annoyances.

●

I was a new teacher when I encountered Helene's parents. The D.'s were a prominent family who knew all the right people. I suspected that Helene's father was sexually abusing her long before I had the nerve to report it. I talked to several other teachers who finally assured me that reporting was the best thing to do. When the local congressman called my principal, I was panic-stricken. I was sure I would lose my job and my reputation. Fortunately my colleagues supported me, and in time the D.'s received the help they needed. The look in Helene's eyes and her new vitality and interest in school were enough to convince me that I'd done the right thing.

●

What, then, if the parents withdraw the child from school or from your classroom? This is always a possibility. But at least you will have involved the family members with the social service system so that the child may be helped. If you are able to talk with the parents and assure them that you wish to be an ally, you may be able to help in the treatment.

Remember that abusive families cry for help in a variety of ways and then often erect smokescreens to cover their cries. Many times no one hears until a child is badly harmed or even killed. Classroom teachers may be in a position to hear these cries for help a little sooner than other members of society. You may be the key to early intervention and a turning point in the life of the family.

Certainly reporting child abuse is neither easy nor clear-cut. But the potential benefit for the abused child is worth every effort you are able to expend.

Teacher's Checklist
for Preparing to Report

1. Have you documented your data and written down the information to organize it in your own mind?

2. Have you analyzed your data? What causes you to suspect abuse/neglect? List the symptoms—physical or behavorial.

3. Have you been able to observe the parent/child interaction? Does the parent see the child as worthwhile or different and/or hard to handle?

4. Have you spoken with other professionals within the school? Do they have reason to suspect abuse/neglect? Why?

5. Do you know the reporting policy of your school? Do you know the answers to the questions on pages 50–51? To whom do you report?

6. Do you have the necessary information required for a report? (See page 53.)

7. Do you (or does the school) have the exact telephone number and address of the agency to which you should report?

8. Have you talked with your administrator about the support you will receive once the report is made? What if the parents try to remove the child from your class? Will you have the support of the administration?

9. Does your school have on hand the necessary report forms?

10. Have you set up a support system for yourself with other teachers or administrators? (After the report is made, you may feel vulnerable and need to talk.)

Now, you should be ready to report, knowing that you are providing a chance for both the child and the family to receive much-needed help.

CHAPTER 5

After the Report

After you have made the report and may perhaps be continuing to validate your data, the social service system will have become involved in the case. This chapter answers some of the questions that teachers have about what happens at this point.

Protective Agency Decisions

When a protective investigation begins, the social worker must make several important decisions. These are discussed in the following pages.

Does the Case Warrant Further Intervention?

In some cases, the intervention of the community may promote improvement. At the other extreme, the social worker may receive no cooperation from the parents, yet have insufficient evidence to ensure court involvement. Some parents are well enough acquainted with the social service system to know exactly what to say or how to look, so that when the social worker visits the home, everything appears to be acceptable. In such cases, it is as frustrating for the social worker as it is for the teacher to close a case before rendering any help. Regardless of your frustration, the best course of action is to offer to keep in touch with the agency so that you can share any further developments. It should also be mentioned that some states require the intervention of a law enforcement agency. (See

Appendix G.) If this is so in your state, the protective agency will know the role the law enforcement agency plays in these cases. Thus the decisions made on behalf of the child may, in fact, be joint decisions of the two agencies.

Is It Safe for the Child to Remain at Home?

Throughout child welfare history, professionals have vacillated between keeping children in their own home and placing them in a foster home. Children feel greater security in their own home, however dysfunctional it may be. Studies have shown that foster home placement does not necessarily ensure a happier life. In fact, for children who are returned to their own home after foster home placement, the situation may deteriorate faster than it would have without placement.

Although the best plan for the child may seem to be removal from a difficult home situation, the social worker may well decide to have the child remain at home and attempt to work with the family intact. Even in cases of sexual abuse, it is more advisable to remove the perpetrator from the home than the child. Needless to say, the exception would be if the child were in immediate danger. Placements may be made either with the voluntary permission of the parents or by court intervention.

Will the Family Receive Help Willingly?

Families may agree to the intervention of a social worker for several reasons:

- They may sincerely want help and have, in fact, been asking for it by their behavior.
- They may fear the legal consequences if they do not agree to be helped.
- They may comply to "get the social worker off their back."

Whatever the motivation, if the agency feels that the family needs help and the family agrees to cooperate, the relationship will probably be voluntary. While this is the preferred treatment, it can sometimes be frustrating if the family does not keep appointments or the old problems begin to reappear. If, on the other hand, the family refuses help initially, or at some point decides not to cooperate any longer, the social worker can opt for court involvement.

Particular instances that require court intervention are as follows:

- The child is in imminent danger of harm.

- Attempts at treatment have failed, and parents have not made progress toward providing adequate care for the child. (8, p. 23)

If there is a decision for court intervention, the social worker files a petition in the juvenile division of the civil court requesting that the family be compelled to get help or that the children be placed in a foster home. This sets in motion a series of procedures that are discussed in Chapter 6.

Whether or not there is court involvement or family cooperation, if the case is assessed to need more help, the agency works with the family. At this point you may be asked to give reports to the social worker concerning your contacts with the family or the child's progress in school.

Exactly What Type of Treatment Does the Family Need?

Family treatment may take several forms:

- concrete services such as financial assistance, medical assistance, housing assistance, day care (to relieve the parent of some stress)

- referral to other services specific to family needs, such as services for special children, family planning, budgeting consultation, counseling

- advocacy services—helping the family to actually obtain the services for which it is eligible
- counseling services (most protective agencies are able to provide these in a limited way; if more in-depth counseling is needed, the family is referred to another source).

Who Will Be Involved in the Treatment of the Family?

The group of professionals concerned with the assessment or treatment of protective situations is often referred to as the Child Protection Team. Some teams are involved only in assessment; others meet for progress reports on the family throughout the treatment. Whether or not there is a formal network, the social worker may involve all or some of the following: health professionals, the child's teacher(s) and perhaps the school nurse, the school social worker, a psychologist, a psychiatric social worker, legal services and other support personnel (from welfare, day care, etc.) as needed, and possibly the child's foster parents, if placement has been indicated. It is most important that all the links of this therapeutic chain remain in contact with one another, bearing in mind that the primary goal is to help the family. Some families may be skillful in building mistrust among professionals. An interesting novel, *The Scofield Diagnosis*, deals with a doctor's attempt to help an abusive family amidst the barriers set up by other professionals (15). Some families may also misinterpret information; as a result mistrust can be built among agencies.

How Long Will Treatment Take?

This is difficult to answer. Many social service agencies set up treatment plans with clients ranging from weeks to months. If the court becomes involved, it may schedule hearings at regular intervals, from six weeks to six months. The severity of the situation may also determine the length of treatment. If the family's prognosis is very poor and few gains are made, the children may be removed. If, on the other hand, the family appears workable, more time may be spent on teaching more effective parenting skills. No abuse or neglect situation can be remedied immediately. The deterioration of family life did not happen overnight.

At What Point Does the Family No Longer Need Services?

The obvious answer depends on the type of child maltreatment:

- In physical abuse, services are terminated when the abuser stops abusing the child and has learned another method of coping with aggressive feelings.

- In neglect, services are terminated when the parent can meet the child's basic needs adequately.

- In sexual abuse, services are terminated when the perpetrator is no longer involved sexually with the child and, ideally, has learned more coping methods to prevent such involvement in the future.

These answers are all that society can realistically offer in these cases, and unfortunately it is difficult to determine if the gains made will be lasting. Some social agencies have arbitrary time limits based upon restrictions of staff time and agency funds. If there is court involvement, the case continues until no further evidence indicates abuse. Few professionals who work with these families are pleased with the criteria used for closing their cases. But until humans become more skilled in understanding and determining human motivation, these are the criteria they must use.

CHAPTER 6

Court
Appearances

•

The first time it was necessary for me to go to court in a juvenile matter, I was apprehensive. I expected to see Perry Mason in all his glory; what I did see was a small courtroom—not unlike a formal classroom—with only a handful of people in attendance.

•

Family or juvenile court sessions are closed, with only the legal staff and the significant people present. No observers may attend and if, in fact, you are asked to serve as a witness, you may be asked to leave the room after your testimony is given.

Suggestions for
a Court Appearance

Your chances of going to court are probably not very great, but it is best to be prepared if you are asked to appear. Protective cases are taken to court if the social worker feels that either the child is in real danger or the family will not cooperate. Prior to any court hearing, the social service agency (or police) files a petition stating that the child is in need of the court's protection. Also, there may be a pretrial hearing to determine if the case can be resolved without court intervention, or if in fact there is enough evidence to go to court. The social service agency then must collect witnesses to substantiate the report. At this point, you may receive a subpoena. In the courtroom there will be no jury, merely a judge, court officers, probation officers, lawyers (for parents, for child, and perhaps for the social service agency), social service personnel, and witnesses. You will merely be asked to state your involvement and any information you may have about the case. One teacher recounts her experience in court and makes some recommendations:

•

As a teacher, I had the opportunity to be a witness in a child neglect hearing. It is very important to bring documentation with you to the hearing. This may include test scores; observations of home conditions; parent and child behavior within the home, and clinical and classroom settings; photographs and dates of home and school contacts. Try to answer each question as truthfully as you can, as you are under oath. In my case, I included not only negative aspects of home conditions and parenting skills, but also positive aspects of the home environment. I answered only when spoken to and did not give my personal opinion on any of the questions asked me.

When testifying, do not sound defensive. As a witness, you are not being judged and you need not fear being interrogated. In my particular situation I was briefed several weeks in advance of the hearing as to the types of questions I might be asked in the courtroom and I was not allowed to hear the other witnesses' testimony during the hearing. If the witnesses are not notified of the results of the hearing, they should contact the social worker involved in the case or the lawyer who is the custodian of the child involved. These professionals should give you the information you want, respecting the rights of confidentiality of all those involved.

•

In addition to these suggestions, it may also be helpful—

- to dress appropriately—considering that courts are conservative.
- to prepare ahead—the documentation of facts, dates, etc., will help you remember.
- not to memorize your testimony—it should sound spontaneous. (8, pp. 49–50)

You may feel somewhat nervous; most people usually do, especially when asked to take an oath. Preparing yourself mentally to answer and concentrating on speaking both loudly and clearly will help (8, pp. 50–51).

The court will be recording your testimony, so it is important that it be clearly audible. If you don't know the answer, don't guess; say you don't know. Although you may be separated from other witnesses, in some cases you may hear their testimony. It is important to present your own story in an organized manner, and to be unafraid to admit your own beliefs.

In some situations you may be asked to appear at a later hearing to update the court on the progress of the child. More than likely, however, you will need to make only one appearance.

Finally, no matter how many times you are asked to appear in court, it should not give you undue anxiety if you remember that you are not on trial. You are merely there to help the child.

CHAPTER 7

How to Help the Child Beyond Reporting

Communicating with the Social Worker

Once child abuse has been reported, the two most important professionals in the child's life are the social worker and the teacher. It is therefore vital that these two key figures work together. Both the social worker who does not consult the teacher and the teacher who does not keep in touch with the social worker miss important information that can help the child as well as each other.

Some teachers have said, "What's the point of reporting? I never heard a thing from the social worker and obviously nothing was done." Not unlike teachers who attempt to give of themselves with skill and understanding to their classes of 30 youngsters, social workers, too, have very large caseloads. Often their attention goes—by necessity—from crisis to crisis with insufficient time for the details of any one case. The neophyte social worker may feel overwhelmed; the overworked, experienced social worker may appear mechanical. But remaining in this profession requires a sincere concern for the welfare of one's clients.

"I may not always get back to teachers as I should," admits an experienced social work-er, "but I really appreciate a phone call letting me know how the child is doing or if anything new has come up with the child or the family."

Although the social worker may be making the major decisions in the child's life, it is the teacher who "lives" with the child day after day whose information can be vital to an agency's treatment plan. Of course the decisions of the social worker are influenced not only by agency policy but also by the court system. A child may be returned to a natural family not because the social worker feels it is the best plan, but because of insufficient evidence for the court to continue custody. In some cases careful documentation by the teacher has been the factor that enabled the social worker and the court to provide a better treatment plan for a child when everyone was convinced that the case should be dismissed.

This is not meant to imply that the responsibility of communication should be solely the teacher's. It is mutual. Both professionals complain of finding it difficult to contact each other. However, most social workers have a day in their offices when they can be reached more easily. And teachers can let social workers know when they have a free period and can be more easily reached by telephone.

Helping the Child Individually

Over the years it becomes clear that abuse and neglect take their toll on a variety of children, usually in similar ways. Abused or neglected children may—

- have a very poor self-image, feeling that they do not matter or that there is something wrong with them.
- need individual attention.
- need to express frustration and anger.
- have unattended educational and medical needs.

78

- need to succeed—to do something right.
- need to know tht they have rights too; those with poor self-image may not know that it is all right to say no to adults.
- have hampered development emotionally, physically, or sexually.

Adults often do not realize that children who are victims of neglect might not understand the messages teachers give them. In her workshop on neglect at the 1985 National Conference on Child Abuse and Neglect, Hendrika Cantwell made an interesting observation. She noted that by the time children go to school, when a teacher says, "Sit in your seats, put your feet on the floor, take out your notebook, and copy the words I put on the board," they are expected to understand such directions. Yet children learn to obey a series of commands through experience. The neglected child who has heard only one command statement, "Sit down" or "Close the door," may have great difficulty absorbing more complex requests (6).

Maltreated youngsters may have another problem with respect to student-teacher communication, Dr. Cantwell points out. Children whose parents are loving and consistent, mature with the acceptance that they are cared about and that adults want what is best for them. They learn to accept adult commands on faith. Therefore when a teacher gives a direction, these children will assume it is for their own good, and will comply. On the other hand, maltreated children, exposed to inconsistent parenting, may not be convinced that adults mean well. When a teacher makes a request, then, such children may refuse to respond because they are unsure if compliance will be in their best interest (6).

It is therefore important that teachers be alert to children's comprehension as well as to their level of trust of adults. During the first few days of class, be especially conscious of how children react to commands. Does each child really seem to know what you want? Further, does a particular child seem to want to please you or seem to comply to avoid punishment?

Some types of assistance for children are more obvious. Referrals for medical testing within the school as well as assessment for special learning needs can be made for any child. Perhaps the two biggest needs—both related—of maltreated children are to improve the self-image and to do "something right." There is also the need to express anger at what has been done to them. Any tasks or exercises that can meet these needs can be helpful. For example, choose tasks that give the youngster a feeling of authority in the classroom or on the playground—something as simple as erasing the chalkboard. Or choose caretaking tasks such as feeding the gerbils. This enables the child to be the caregiver and to learn ways to properly care for something or someone as well as to feel important. And a quiet word of approval upon completion of the task may mean a great deal to the abused or neglected child. It is of course important to rotate key tasks so that one child does not seem to be favored.

High school students can also be given tasks of importance. In each class, the teacher has an opportunity to comment on the student's little successes as they are accomplished. For some older children, the sports area is a natural outlet. Shooting a few baskets amidst quips about life and happenings at school may be the perfect occasion for building trust by encouraging the youngster to focus on the positive or attainable elements of his or her life.

The high school years also provide an excellent opportunity to help students assess their strengths in the interest of career goals—with coaxing perhaps from a guidance counselor, a concerned teacher, or a coach. Several programs are available to help teens not focused on college—either because of financial reasons, lack of motivation, or self-concept—assess and prepare themselves for some type of job. These programs—such as Jobs for

80

America's Graduates (1250 I Street, NW, Washington, DC 20005)—not only help students explore strengths and weaknesses, they also train them in resume writing, job searching, interviewing, and getting along with others in a work setting. Such skills can be invaluable to a child whose emotional growth and ambition may have been stunted by abuse and neglect.

The high school years seem to be the time when many young people are looking for a mentor. Perhaps one of the greatest benefits the teacher can offer those in this age group, other than helping them discover themselves, is to be open and approachable as a person—that is, to communicate that you will hear them if they need to talk.

●

A high school teacher enrolled in my "Sexual Abuse" course carried her text to school, at first unwittingly, intending to read it during her study period. Many students never noticed the book, but several who did asked questions and eventually were able to talk with her regarding abuse they had suffered. Besides making referrals to help these youngsters, this teacher was able to stand by her students in a way that told them that she was there if they needed her again.

●

Some students, teens or younger, are not so easily helped. The behavior of disruptive children may need to be dealt with firmly, but with increased understanding. Unfortunately the school's frequent disciplinary tool is suspension, one of the worst things that could happen to an abused or neglected child. And the use of corporal punishment—already prohibited in several states and discouraged in most others—is also highly undesirable for these children. A more effective method is to point out the positive benefits of acceptable behavior, at the same time motivating the children to accept responsibility for their actions and also to feel deserving of any rewards that may result. For a good illustration of this technique in use, see *Marva*

Collins' Way, the story of an educator with a real skill in getting through to children considered problems (12, p. 20).

Children who have been abused need to feel that they have alternatives and the rewards of their choices. Or, whether destructive or withdrawn, they may just need time to talk about what has happened to them. The informed teacher can be their best ally. Understanding through reading and/ or training what has happened to the child can be of invaluable help in knowing what to say. Sensitivity to clues that the child needs to talk—such as a change of behavior or attitude—is important.

Certain exercises can give children an opportunity to share their feelings. For example, "On My Mind" encourages students to draw silhouettes of themselves and then "cut out words, pictures, etc., that represent their personal thoughts, thus making a collage of their current concerns" (48). This type of exercise not only gives children an opportunity to express feelings or concerns, but it helps them realize that their feelings *are* important. In addition, teachers of younger children can use puppets or other toys to enable youngsters to voice their own feelings.

Helping the Child in the Classroom

The average teacher may not have time for more individual help or may not want to single out a child. It is possible, however, to help the abused or neglected child within the classroom with resulting benefit to the whole class. Such help can accomplish several purposes:

- It enhances the self-image and feelings of worth not only of the abused or neglected child, but of classmates as well.

- It enables classmates to understand the abused or neglected child.

- It stimulates other reports and educates children in areas relating to abuse and neglect.

The type of exercise used in the classroom may be general or specific. For example, all children may participate in an activity designed to enhance self-image or they may view a film geared specifically toward preventing abuse or encouraging the reporting of abuse.

Enhancing Self-Image and Feelings of Worth

Wells and Canfield cite numerous exercises, many of which can help a child feel important. They use such topics as "My Strength," "Who Am I?" "Accepting My Body," and "Where Am I Going?" to help the child develop a better concept of self (48). Other exercises in this area include discussions such as "What's the Best Thing About Me?" or in the case of high-school-age students, "What Have I Accomplished About Which I Am Most Proud?" These discussions are good ways not only to discern the quality of the individual's self-image, but also to help improve it. Class projects in which all members have a part are also useful to help children feel needed.

Other helpful books include *Personalizing Education: Values Clarification and Beyond* (28), *Teaching Children to Love Themselves* (33), and *Left-Handed Teaching: Lessons in Affective Education* (7).

How else can you help the child in class? Use any activity that encourages children to think in terms of their own potential rather than of their limitations. Such exercises can help both abused and neglected children and their classmates think more of themselves. Or begin in another way. Even though it may be difficult with some children, look for their positive attributes and strengths. A mental exercise searching out these strengths may be good with a particular child who may be especially trying or unpopular with other students.

Once you have a sense of the positive aspects of this child, encourage those features. Granted, if in a class of 30 children you begin to accentuate the positive aspects of one abused or neglected child, the remainder of the class may react. You may therefore want to acknowledge the strengths of all the children, enlisting their help to discover their own strengths in the form of a game, for example. (Several such games are listed in the books just mentioned.) Or first ask the children to think about the "good things" about themselves. Keep in mind that children with poor self-images may have difficulty identifying positive points about themselves and may need gentle coaxing or suggestions. The fact that an adult, especially an authority figure, is able to see that they do anything well may be the first step toward increased trust between you and these children and may perhaps begin to move them toward the development of a better self-image.

Sometimes you can ask students to write autobiographies, and through this means help them recognize the positive aspects of their lives as well as of themselves. For a child whose life story is punctuated with pain, there can always be positives if one looks for them. For example, Robbie (mentioned in Chapter 1 as a neglected child) was becoming aware that he received little of his parents' attention. Yet as a caretaker of younger siblings, he could be helped to realize his great importance to them. It might also be helpful to emphasize to Robbie how responsible it is of him to come to school every day. Admittedly in such a case you would be overlooking negatives—such as the possible stealing, the hygiene—but as you begin to improve Robbie's image of himself, you would have his trust and attention in teaching the class about hygiene, for example, or arranging a school lunch for him, or teaching him to make lunch himself if any supplies were available at home.

Remember that abused and neglected children probably live in a world of negatives at home. Emphasizing their positive aspects may be difficult for them to handle at first, but with practice, the effect may even transfer into the home.

It is perhaps more difficult to help the high school student in the classroom setting because of the constantly changing environment—class membership, subject, etc. Some subjects, however, lend themselves to self-exploration and enhancement of self-image. For example, you can use a literature course to look at the role of women in literature, emphasizing not only the author's message, characterization, and plot, but also the strengths portrayed by women. This can lead to an opportunity to help the female (and perhaps male) class members assess their own strengths. Health or family life courses can lead more obviously to looking at the self and individual potential. Peer support groups are another vehicle to help teens with adolescent/self-image issues. Adolescence, a natural period of self-exploration, can prove a perfect time to introduce positive concepts and role models.

A vital part of improving the self-image is helping the child feel competent in a number of ways. Children with limited experiences at home have not developed to their fullest. Linda V. Williams in her book *Teaching for the Two-Sided Mind* (49) suggests that it is important to teach children in a way that allows them to learn with the whole brain—using both left and right hemispheres. This concept is especially important for children who have lacked stimulation at home.

To Touch or Not to Touch

Teachers contemplating the use of sexual abuse prevention materials in their classrooms have asked me whether all the emphasis on abuse will not discourage teachers from touching. Recently a major TV network called me with the same concern.

In fact, touching can be an important part of learning. Studies of parenting and maternal deprivation tell us that touching is vital from the first hours of bonding and throughout life. A hug is associated with support and love. A touch of the hand, a pat on the back are signals that someone cares. But does encouraging children to be aware of "bad touch" frighten teachers away from touching?

I believe that teachers should not be afraid of touching—if they lay the "groundwork." This groundwork involves some basic education for children. Today's sexual abuse prevention materials teach children about good, bad, and confusing touch. "Good touch" is a hug—if that feels good—a pat, or a variety of indicators that a child is doing well or that someone likes the child. "Bad touch" is usually first described by children as hitting, punching, pinching, or any touch that hurts. That definition can be expanded to include "anything that doesn't feel good to the child." For example, adults may enjoy ruffling a child's hair—a seemingly harmless gesture for the adults—but for children who do not like having their hair ruffled, it is "bad touch." "Confusing touch" is something one is not sure about. If teachers also help children recognize that parts of their body are private (for young children these parts can be explained as those covered by a bathing suit), there may be less confusion. Children who are confused about a particular type of touch should be encouraged to ask adults about it.

This brings us to the second part of the groundwork. After teaching children to recognize types of touch, teachers then must encourage them to express their feelings about these touches. If someone touches them in a way they do not like, children should be encouraged to say so—preferably to the person touching—or at least to another adult. If the little boy whose hair was ruffled does not like it, he should be given "permission" to tell the person who ruffled it about his reaction. By the same token, the adult must respect the child's wishes. This will also encourage children to acknowledge good touch and to express their feelings: "I like it when you hug me, Miss Jones. It makes me feel warm inside."

Empowering children to recognize types of touching and to be able to express their feelings allows teachers to touch with more confidence. Of course there will always be children who do not like being touched. It is hoped that they will tell teachers this. Some teachers may prefer not to touch. That, too, is their personal choice.

Touching should not be a problem for teachers. The key is to know how to have open communication with students about their feelings about being touched and the teachers' feelings about touching.

Helping Classmates Understand the Abused or Neglected Child

Children find it difficult to understand why a particular child disrupts a classroom or antagonizes peers. Even more incomprehensible to the more outgoing child is the quiet, withdrawn student who seems removed from the classroom environment. The way in which the abused or neglected child chooses to deal with peers may greatly affect the peers' responses.

Perhaps a starting point is to educate the class about feelings, emotions, and even abuse, including the feelings that an abused person may have. This can be done simply by presenting "What-if" statements to which children respond. For example, "What if a friend breaks your favorite toy?" or "What if your mother hits you very hard?" Once children explore the range of possible feelings in response to these statements, they will be able to better understand the feelings of others.

For withdrawn children, you might encourage other students to include them in their games. Making such a request of a more outgoing or empathetic child may prove the most successful.

If children are disruptive, the chances are they are disturbing their classmates. Students will frequently handle the situation themselves if given a chance, but a lesson in empathetic response can change the "Aw, keep still, Johnny!" to "You're a nice kid, and I hate to see you have everyone mad at you by . . ." Children respond to their environment. They will imitate the teacher who employs an empathetic approach.

Hygiene problems can also be handled by peers. In one case a high school student patiently counseled a peer on the need for bathing to acquire more friends. A few years ago, the norm was "the dirtier the better" but the importance of designer jeans somehow emphasizes a clean body. Thus cleanliness can help students feel more acceptable.

The high school student whose primary goal is to be "one of the gang" may find it more difficult to step away from the crowd and help a peer. If a benevolent student cannot be found, peer support groups set up by the guidance office can sometimes be useful in communicating acceptance to an otherwise outcast teenager. Again, education can be the key. Teenagers may be more empathetic if they perceive the reason for a classmate's problem.

Stimulating Other Reports

There are a variety of ways to encourage reporting. Specific filmstrips such as *Sometimes It's Okay to Tattle* and *Some Secrets Should Be Told* talk to younger children about abuse and sexual abuse. *Child Abuse: Don't Hide the Hurt* discusses latency for preteens. *Who Do You Tell?* prepares children (7 to 12 years of age) for reporting abuse and also aids them in knowing where to go in other emergencies. (See Appendix I.)

The use of audiotapes such as *A Dragon in My Closet* (for young children about physical abuse) or *Deborah Wore Designer Jeans* (for older children about sexual abuse) may generate discussion about abuse as well as about whom to tell when children feel they have problems. (Both audiotapes are available separately from NEA and are included in *Child Abuse and Neglect: The NEA Multimedia Training Program.*)

In addition, there are training programs geared to personal safety and prevention of sexual abuse. These programs address a variety of developmental issues such as privacy and assertiveness as well as abuse. Books for children such as *Red Flag, Green Flag People* or *My Very Own Book About Me* can be used as workbooks to aid students' understanding of how to prevent sexual abuse. Such tools may also stimulate reports. (See Appendix I.)

As a way of understanding, educating, and encouraging reports, children can be asked to write puppet shows or plays telling about abuse. One sixth grade class, with help from a local social agency, wrote a play on what to do if a friend is abused. Then the class presented it to the school. The result was overwhelming. The door was opened. Not only was the class better informed, but other children within the school felt better able to self-report.

Here, too, it may be helpful to educate children in issues relating to abuse and neglect such as hygiene. For years advertisers of toothpastes and soaps have made their products more appealing by animation and dramatization. Some free programs may be available through these companies for classroom use, or all the children can do a project on hygiene to create more sensitivity in the entire group and to prevent any one child from being singled out.

Sex education is an area fraught with controversy. Is it the responsibility of the parent or the school? The fact is that many children have much misinformation about sexual concepts. Surprisingly, sexually abused children may be equally misinformed. They may have been taken beyond their years in sexual activity but lack knowledge of normal experience. In addition, children need to be taught about their bodies in general, with emphasis on appreciating them.

A variety of other topics can also help abused and neglected children and their classmates. A quick perusal of the symptoms listed in Chapters 1 and 2 may bring more of these to mind.

Helping the Foster Child in the Classroom

Foster children may need a special kind of concern from their teachers. You may find in your classroom a student who has been removed from home for protective reasons and lives in a foster home. This child may present special problems. The biggest issue that the foster child is probably working out is that of separation and loss. No matter how difficult the home situation, this child has experienced the loss of an important element of life. The expression of this loss may differ from individual to individual. One child may be withdrawn or sullen, another difficult, exhibiting behavior problems. Feelings of inconstancy and instability may create a child who seems not to care. The best way to deal with these situations is to contact the social worker and insist on being told something of the child's background. The youngster may have special needs or interests that you can address. Mostly, however, foster children are wondering if you will reject or abandon them as others seem to have done. They may test you or tell wild, unbelievable stories to shock you. Knowledge of their background may help here too. The need to know that they are all right, no matter what the family situation, is paramount for these youngsters. Again the classroom teacher can be not only an ally, but also an important source of information on the child's progress by maintaining close contact with the social worker and the foster parents.

Any discussion of help for foster children would be remiss without mentioning the importance of foster parents. These people as a group may be victims of misconceptions. The vast majority, greatly overworked and grossly underpaid, are concerned, dedicated individuals who take their job seriously. As one foster mother put it:

When a child is placed in a foster home, the foster parents take on many roles. . . . The formal professional

90

role of the child protective team is essential but the informal daily role of the foster parent is at the root of the child's progress. It is the foster parent who makes the majority of appointments, who must screen the child for possible problems, with resulting treatments after discussions and consultation with professional staff. Bypassing the foster parent's role in the treatment of the "trauma of child abuse and neglect" is like bypassing the electrical outlet in the operation of any electrical apparatus. The foster parent is the link between the many forces involved in this endeavor.

Frequent contact with the foster parents can help the teacher understand what is happening in the child's homelife and provide them with information concerning the child's progress in school. Through the foster parents the teacher can learn of any new treatments that may have altered the child's behavior in the school setting. A note, a telephone call, or an appointment with these caretakers can ensure the more harmonious orchestration of the child's already out-of-tune life.

Whether keeping in touch with the child's natural or surrogate parents, aiding the social service team, or daily contacts in the classroom, the influence of the teacher on an abused or neglected child is profound. In many cases the teacher is the second most influential person in the child's life—one whose membership on the treatment team is vital.

CHAPTER 8

The Child's Family

Current newspapers and magazines are full of statistics attesting to the "vicious mal-treatment of children by their parents." Yet the sensationalistic drama of these statistics distorts the picture of the disraught human being behind the abuse. Admittedly, teachers who see the evidence of child abuse and neglect find it difficult to imagine that anyone could relate to children in such ways. However, except for an inability to deal with life in cases of extremes, the parents of these child victims are not unlike other people.

This chapter contains profiles of the physically abusive parent, the neglectful parent, the sexually abusive parent, and the emotionally abusive parent. Individual parents may not fit these profiles exactly. But in most cases enough of the characteristics are usually present so that teachers can use these guidelines for recognition.

The Physically Abusive Parent

•

Libby Carter was a neat, well-dressed young woman whose house appeared immaculate—to the few who had seen it. Libby, her husband, and two children had recently moved and she reported knowing few people. Deeper exploration of Libby's family background would have revealed that she had married young and had had an extremely difficult time in her pregnancies, especially with Tommy, her first child. As a baby, Tommy had been colicky and difficult, and Libby, an only child, had felt at a loss to know what to do. Her husband, Mike, a hard-working, conservative man, expected her to know what to do. He often brought work home and was annoyed when

Tommy's crying made it difficult to concentrate. In addition, the couple never seemed to be able to make ends meet, which caused a great deal of friction between them.

●

This may not seem to be an unusual scenario in an age of unpredictable economy and increased mobility. However, Libby Carter was brought to the attention of the local protective agency because five-year-old Tommy repeatedly came to school with unexplained bruises.

Any parent will readily admit that there are times when a child becomes so exasperating that it may be difficult not to lash out in anger. Most parents, however, are able to maintain control so that they do not abuse their children or punish them excessively. Somewhere they have learned how to maintain control. Dr. Ray Helfer described physically abusive individuals as those whose experiences with their own parents have not provided adequate preparation to become parents themselves. In short, they have not learned five vital elements.*

1. Abusive parents have not learned appropriate ways to have their needs met.

Helfer used the scenario of the child who asks a question while the parent is on the telephone. The parent continues the conversation and the child becomes more insistent. Instead of simply answering, "I'll be with you in a minute," the parent continues to ignore the child until the request becomes a tantrum. Then the parent responds. Eventually the child learns to do away with the earlier steps and just has the tantrum. As an adult this translates into overreactions to have needs met.

2. Abusive parents have not learned the difference between feelings and actions.

If a parent consistently strikes out in anger rather than verbalizing the anger, the child

---

*These tasks were discussed in a lecture given by Dr. Helfer, in New Bedford, Mass., in March 1979. They are adapted with permission.

learns that anger equals aggression or hitting. As an adult this individual may hit when angry instead of recognizing the anger and treating it in a different way.

3. Abusive parents have not learned to make decisions.

It stands to reason that if control is an issue in abusive situations, the abuser feels out of control. Most parents give their children chances to make decisions without even thinking about it. "Would you like peanut butter and jelly or bologna in your lunchbox tomorrow?" Children whose lives are so thoroughly structured that they are not allowed to make any decisions begin to feel powerless and this feeling may transfer into later life.

Helfer also pointed out that children should be given opportunities to make decisions appropriate to their role. For example, it is not so much "Do you want to go to bed?" as "Which foot would you like to put on the stair first, on your way to bed?"

4. Abusive parents have not learned that they are responsible for their own actions and not for the actions of others.

Have you ever known a child whose parent communicates in grief and bitterness that an absent spouse (perhaps too immature to handle the problems of parenting) would not have left the home if it had not been for the child? In such cases the child begins to feel responsible for the pain others are experiencing.

At the same time, if not taught otherwise, the child may begin to deny responsibility for deeds or misdeeds. The classic response of the two- or three-year-old, "The dog did it," becomes internalized so that as an adult the individual feels powerless and becomes convinced that whatever the offense, it was in fact caused by the action of another person.

5. Abusive parents have not learned to delay gratification.

Children naturally want instant satisfaction of their desires. But as they are guided through development, they come to realize that some pleasures must be delayed. Adults who have not learned this lesson want instant results—immediate obedience from their children or immediate solutions to their problems. When the act or solution does not ensue directly, the individual feels out of control and may react negatively.

Parents who have not learned these tasks in their own childhood may not teach them to their offspring. Thus there is a pattern—many abusive parents were themselves abused as children. This is not to say that every maltreated child will become an abusive adult. One of the keys to interrupt the cycle seems to be insight and learning these identified tasks in later life. Helfer also contends that the learning of these tasks should be a necessary part of any treatment program. His *Childhood Comes First: A Crash Course in Childhood for Adults* was written to help parents learn these tasks (26).

In addition to inadequate preparation for parenting, environmental factors may play a part in the drama of abuse. Often physically abusive parents may experience the following:

- frequent geographic moves
- financial stresses such as uncertain employment, changes in employment, or underemployment
- other types of stresses.

Also at high risk are parents in situations that include

- marriage at a very young age
- pregnancy before or shortly after marriage
- difficult labor and delivery
- abusive families during their own childhood
- marital difficulties.

In short, the lives of abusive parents are characterized by a great many stresses. The parents themselves usually present a picture of

- social isolation
- excessive neatness
- unrealistically high expectations for children
- role reversal with children (i.e., the child parents the parent and often does a great many parental tasks such as housework and child care)
- poor control of children (especially older children)
- inability to cope with crises.

Unusually high expectations can be seen frequently in abusive families. Parents look to their offspring as extensions of themselves and as somehow responsible for proving that they are worthwhile. Failure to meet parental expectations convinces the children that they are of little worth—a feeling which, with ripple effect, creates a feeling of failure in the parents as well. The diagram of the vicious cycle of physical abuse depicts this self-perpetuating phenomenon.

Adolescent Abuse

Adolescent abuse may, in some instances, differ from the abuse of younger children. And the motivations of the parents, in turn, may differ as well. There are three types of adolescent abuse:

1. Abuse that begins in childhood and continues through adolescence.
2. Abuse that may begin in childhood, such as spankings, but intensifies in adolescence.
3. Abuse that begins in adolescence and is directly related to the problems of adolescence (19, p. 5)

The first type of adolescent abuse is based on too high, unmet parental expectations.

VICIOUS CYCLE OF PHYSICAL ABUSE

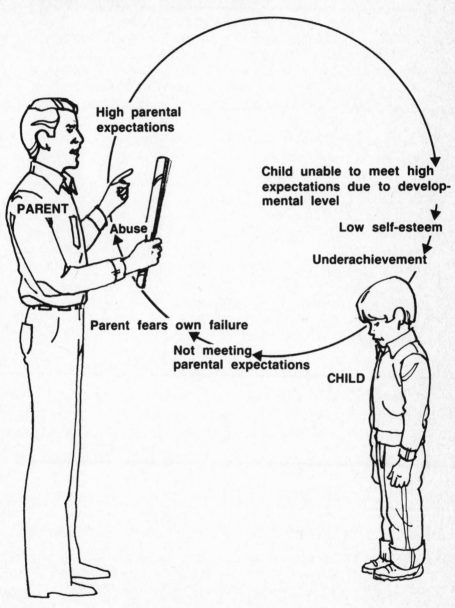

High parental expectations

PARENT

Abuse

Parent fears own failure

Not meeting parental expectations

Child unable to meet high expectations due to developmental level

Low self-esteem

Underachievement

CHILD

Because these unrealistic expectations are not being met, the parents feel that they are failures as parents. The abuse that is perpetrated against a young child up to 7 years of age may let up slightly during the otherwise quiet latency years (7 to 11) but may be stimulated again during the turbulent teens. Thus there is a pattern of continuing, though fluctuating, abuse.

The second type of adolescent abuse is related to control. During childhood the family accepts and uses corporal punishment, which appears to compel the child into acceptable behavior. As the child grows in stature and independence, however, this type of punishment is ineffective. At the same time, the older parent begins to feel more and more out of control of the situation and abuse ensues.

This abusive behavior intensifies in adolescence. While the young child could be subdued by threats over control or belittlement, the adolescent tests, to the point that the parent feels that only physical means will suffice. Emotions by this time have usually reached a fever pitch and abuse is the outcome.

The third type of adolescent abuse becomes obvious in the following:

●

Mary had been a model child and an excellent student just as her mother before her had been. Mary's mother, who was remembered by some of the older teachers in the small town school, had had a brilliant school career and had gone on to college, eventually marrying later in life. An only child, Mary had always been doted upon by her parents. Now in high school, her popularity was assured by her open, jovial manner. She was quite confident and appeared very much her own person. At the beginning of her junior year, however, the teachers were much surprised by the change in Mary. She became sullen, difficult, and verbally abusive to peers and teachers alike. So concerned was the school counselor that she asked Mary's parents to come to school. Sensing a definite change in the family atmosphere, the counselor asked that the family seek outside counseling. The counseling eventually revealed that Mary's mother, once an outgoing, popular girl like her daughter, was feeling emotionally unsupported and worthless. Watching her daughter's beauty and sexuality wax as her own waned became too much for this insecure woman. Feeling totally out of control of the situation, she struck out at Mary who, in her distorted view, appeared as the cause of her turmoil.

●

While an adolescent is blossoming into adulthood, the parent may be looking forward only to retirement, seeing her or his life being lived again through the child and yet feeling powerless to control it. This period has been called "change of life" and sometimes "middlescence," denoting the adult in midyears battling the same identity issues as the adolescent offspring, with perhaps not as much to look forward to. Fisher, et al. cite three family patterns in which parents are working through issues at the same time as their children:

1. Abuse may be related to the working through of the developmental issue of sexuality. The father may be aroused by his daughter's blossoming, feel guilty and reject or strike out against his daughter. He may also project his guilt upon her boyfriends, accusing them of taking advantage of his daughter. The same pattern may operate with mothers and their sons. Uncontrolled, these feelings could escalate to abuse.

2. Abuse may be related to fears about separation. Parents who dote on their children in childhood may not be prepared for the turbulence of adolescence. Sporadic incidents of testing behavior, as the teen attempts to explore independence, may provoke abuse. Frequently the adolescent feels forced into making a drastic break from the family setting (running away, for example).

3. Abuse may be a result of the parents' needs to work through their own unresolved adolescent issues. Parents feeling in competition with the child may participate in peer-like fights.

The rivalry may even take on overtones of sexuality, as between daughter and divorced mother. The adolescent may also be "set up" to act out against authority figures as the parent never dared. Parents feeling conflict over their own inner pulls and their son's or daughter's behavior may respond to the child abusively. (19, pp. 40–41)

Whatever the family dynamics, this type of adolescent abuse results from the conflict between the developmental stages of adolescence and middlescence.

Abusive parents of young children or adolescents are fearful of disclosure and racked with guilt. They fear censure and often have nowhere to turn. In the life of the average, relatively happy individual, friends and a social life are an integral part of everyday experience. More often than not, the abusive parent lacks these contacts and has few friends to turn to in a crisis. This parent does not have a support system and thus feels isolated, alone, and unable to function in a healthy way.

Unfortunately the problems of abusive parents may have repercussions. Their inability to handle emotions appropriately may be transferred to older offspring. It is not unusual to find a teenager who reflects such parental behavior by abusing a younger sibling.

It should also be noted that some apparent examples of parental abuse may not be what they seem. As pointed out in the discussion of physical abuse in Chapter 1, some children exhibit evidence of certain cultural customs that appear to be indicators of abuse or neglect. Awareness of cultural differences and careful observation can help teachers distinguish between these two situations.

The importance of this distinction is demonstrated by a 1983 ruling by the Maryland Court of Special Appeals:

•

In this case a child newly arrived in the United States from the Central African Republic was placed in a foster home after county officials, investigating doctors' reports of scars on the child's body, decided she was a victim of child abuse. The child's father insisted that his daughter's wounds resulted from cuts from the tall, sharp grasses common to his country and from a doctor's use of a heated cow's horn to treat the cuts.

In its ruling, the intermediate court decided: "There is a serious question whether the evidence in this case warrants so drastic a disposition as to have removed [the child] from her home. . . . There was not the slightest evidence that the parents, either of them, had abused the child."

•

The Neglectful Parent

The neglectful parent shares certain characteristics with the abusive parent such as poor self-image and role reversal with the child. In other areas, there are marked differences. While almost compulsive order and cleanliness may characterize the life of the abusive parent, the life of the neglectful parent is practically devoid of routine or consistency, and issues such as cleanliness have little import.

The overwhelming desire of neglectful parents is to meet their unmet needs, which are tragic remnants of their own childhood neglect. The most obvious characteristic of these individuals is a lack of constructive energy. They may be apathetic or hostile, and appear to lack the ability to parent constructively.

Neglectful parents may or may not have a support system. For these who do, however, it is often a deviant subculture of other neglectful parents.

---

*Ecological refers to social context in relation to degenerating neighborhoods, etc., which attract people with similar lifestyles.

According to Polansky, Chalmers, Buttenweiser, and Williams, theorists have attributed neglect to a variety of causes:

...the economic, emphasizing the role of material deprivation and poverty; the ecological,* in which a family's background is seen as responsive to the larger social context in which it is embedded; and the personalistic, which attributes poor child care to individual differences among parental personalities, particularly their character structures. (39, p. 21)

The authors of this study (which emphasized mothers because fathers were not always available) lean toward the personalistic or developmental failures in parents. They cited several parental subcategories: "the apathetic-futile; the impulse-ridden; the mentally retarded; the woman in reactive depression; and the woman who is borderline or even psychotic, which is rare . . ." (39, p. 38). Social workers work with many clients whom these authors described as "women who appeared passive, withdrawn, lacking in expression" (39, p. 39). Also, these women were characterized by—

- a feeling that nothing was worth doing (for example, "What's the point of changing the baby's diaper, he'll only wet it again?")
- an emotional numbness or lack of affect that may be mistaken for depression
- superficial relationships where the needy individual desperately clings to another
- a lack of competence in basic daily living skills compounded by a fear of failure if they tried to learn these skills
- a passive expression of anger through hostile compliance
- a general negative attitude
- a hampered ability to problem solve, making verbal accessibility to others difficult
- a perhaps unconscious ability to make others feel as negative and depressed as they do. (39, pp. 39–40)

Consider the following example:

●

Mrs. Benner was a 25-year-old mother of five children: Ralphie, 6 years; Eddie, 3 years; Susan, 20 months; and twins, Terry and Gerry, 6 months. The Benner family was reported by Ralphie's teacher who was concerned about his rotting teeth, extremely dirty appearance, and the fact that he appeared to have a good deal of child care responsibility despite his age. Shortly after the report, the twins were hospitalized for malnutrition.

The Benner house was in extremely poor condition with a strong smell of urine and little visible evidence of food. Mrs. Benner greeted the social worker in a torn, dirty housecoat and although she talked, she had an aura of passive hostility. Susan was standing at the bars in a nearby crib, clad only in a soiled undershirt. When asked why the baby was not diapered, Mrs. Benner responded that she'd only have to be changed. The crib sheet was torn and had been urinated upon numerous times.

Although Mrs. Benner was apparently highly dependent upon her live-in boyfriend, their relationship consisted of watching TV and frequenting the local pub—leaving Ralphie to care for the other children. Mrs. Benner had little sense of housekeeping or child care and no idea of how to use the food she received from the community agency. Any attempts to help her cook creatively with this food or to clean and care for her children were met with a sullen response of noncompliance. Only the threat of the children's removal eventually elicited some positive response.

●

In addition to the Polansky et al. typology, neglectful parents exhibit the following traits:

- an inability to recognize or meet their children's needs
- an attempt to escape through alcohol, drugs, or sexual promiscuity
- frequent instances of single parent families
- possible history of deviant behavior
- isolation from the larger community and its resources

- a childlike demeanor
- a burden of physical and psychological ailments.

Frequently the neglectful parent's life represents a history of generations living in disorder, poverty, and neglect. These parents have not learned during their own childhood how to parent effectively. Perhaps they have never felt that anyone outside their own little network cares about them. In working with Mrs. Benner, for example, the social worker's task will be a difficult one. If the decision is made to let the children remain in the home, it will be necessary to communicate to the mother that someone does care; that her problems will not so totally overwhelm this helper that she will once again be left alone. Beyond the establishment of trust with a representative of the community, she can be put in touch with other community resources such as visiting nurses, financial aid, day care, fuel assistance, teaching of homemaker skills, which will greatly enhance her lifestyle. In other words, treatment of neglectful parents consist largely of "parenting the parents" so that they can learn to parent their children.

The Sexually Abusive Parent

Although parents teach their children to beware of strangers, it is not the stranger who presents the greatest danger. Seventy to 85 percent (depending upon the source) of sexual abusers are known to the child, and at least one half of that percentage may be a relative or a family member.

If a child is molested by someone he or she does not know, it is vital that both the child and the family help to prevent the child from internalizing the trauma and the family from unconsciously perpetuating it by denial. The same is true if the child is molested by an acquaintance or more distant relative.

Who in fact is the perpetrator of a sexual abuse? Most abusers (97 percent) are male (14, p. 38). They are likely to choose either girls or boys according to their typology. Girls, however, are more frequent victims.

A. Nicholas Groth, well known for his work with sexual offenders, cites several characteristics that he has seen demonstrated by these offenders. Such an offender may—

- appear more submissive than assertive, especially in relationships. He may see himself as a victim and not in control of his life.

- feel isolated; a loner who does not belong in relationship to others.

- feel fearful, depressed, and doubtful of his own worth, rejected by the outside world.

- not seem to be able to derive pleasure from or feel security in life—thus causing him to replace adults with a child who symbolizes his own immaturity. (24, pp. 229–30)

Groth explains further that the offender's insecurities appear as either aggression and dominance in his family or passivity and dependence. For example, Mr. Daniels and Mr. Walker, both members of the local PTA, were in direct contrast with each other.

●

Mr. Daniels, a long-time PTA president, was outspoken, aggressive, and highly verbal. He ruled his retiring wife and two daughters with a stern hand. For those who knew him, his aggressiveness better masked a profound sense of insecurity. It became obvious that beyond a superficial directing relationship with adults, he could not cope with any more equal liaison. His unrelenting overstrictness with his eldest teenage daughter was eventually brought to the attention of school officials, resulting in the final disclosure of their incestuous relationship.

Mr. Walker was the new husband of Thelma Walker, another assertive individual. He was as shy as his wife was outgoing, creating an interesting contrast. Through marriage he had inherited several young sons who were unlike their mother and as retiring as their new stepfather. It was not until several years after the marriage that school officials learned through other children that mild-mannered Mr. Walker was sexually abusing his eight-year-old stepson.

•

Groth divides sexual offenders into two categories: fixated and regressed. Those in the fixated category exhibit the following characteristics:

- an interest in children that started during adolescence
- main interest in children as opposed to adults
- more likely to molest boys
- great difficulty in relating to peers
- overwhelmed by the logistics of life
- sexually victimized as children (true of about 50 percent of offenders) at about the same age as their child victims
- relationships with women usually initiated by women
- chaotic childhood with numerous moves, illnesses, or parental marriage problems
- frequently seem like children to their wives
- show little or no guilt for the sexual abuse. (42, pp. 99–104)

The fixated abuser usually chooses boys becasue he sees himself in them and mentally lowers himself to their level. He perceives himself at the same maturity level as his victim and therefore a peer. Although this offender may also choose a girl victim, he views her in much the same way. In short, he tries to join with his victim, seeking the undemanding love he feels he did not receive as a child. The regressed offender may have developed normally as far as sexual preference is concerned, but has found adult relationships and lifestyle beyond his ability to cope. Most often this offender is married, has done fairly well with peers to this point, and has carried out his role as an adult adequately. His present life may be wrought with stress such as unemployment, marital problems, moves, crises, sudden sexual dysfunction, new disability (retirement or aging). Unlike the fixated offender, he does not necessarily premeditate the relationship. It is more a case of something that "just happened" in his mind. Thus there is a scenario of a man who—

- has a primary interest in agemates.
- has a recently developed interest in children.
- may have begun abusing impulsively.
- is under a lot of stress.
- continues to have sexual experiences with adults as well as with children.
- may be more likely to be involved with alcohol.
- is attracted to girl victims.
- is usually married. (42, pp. 104–9)

Although not every offender fits neatly into Groth's categories, his typologies are widely used and at least help us begin to understand the complex personality of the abuser.

The regressed abuser chooses children because they offer a nonconflictual, undemanding relationship of warm, mutual dependence and love. He elevates the child to his age level, seeing her as more mature and womanly. He too is seeking the all-loving relationship that will give him a feeling of importance.

What part does this abuser play in the child's life? He may be a relative, a friend of the family, a neighbor, a babysitter, or even a father. (Some cases of mother-son or mother-daughter incest have been reported, but usually the incestuous parent is the father.) Blair and Rita Justice discuss the incestuous father (somewhat overlapping Groth's ideas on characteristics of the abuser) in *The Broken Taboo: Sex in the Family* (29). Along with the

introvert and the tyrant, they mention another moti-
vational type called the rationalizer. This individual
rationalizes that his incestuous involvement with his
daughter is based upon his desire to teach her about
sex, his deep love for her, his desire to protect her
from others who may use her for sexual purposes; or
in some cases the father believes in total sexual
freedom in the home (29, pp. 62–80).

Whatever the typology of the father,
how does the mother fit into this complex domestic
puzzle? Why would she "stand by" allowing her
daughter to be abused? Some theorists feel that on
some level—either conscious or unconscious—the
mother knows about the relationship or at least
suspects and cannot bring herself to admit her fears.
This mother usually—

- depends financially or emotionally upon her
  husband.
- participates in role reversal with her daughter so
  that the girl has taken much of the responsibility
  from the mother.
- satisfies the basic needs of her children, but may
  not be participating in nurturing.
- is seen by her daughter as having failed the father.
- has a strained and unsuccessful relationship with
  her daughter.
- is absent at prime nurturing hours such as bed-
  time. (Her absence may take the form of illness,
  working long hours or late, or being involved in
  activities outside the home.)
- has a poor self-image.
- fails to set limits in her home.
- has unreasonable expectations of her husband and
  children (may expect them to nurture her).
- may have been abused as a child herself.
- may not be interested or enjoyably involved in a
  sexual relationship with her husband. (42, pp.
  172–81; 44, pp. 195–202)

Like her husband, the mother may be either dominant or dependent. In rare cases, when it is the mother who is the abuser and the father who stands aside, the characteristics of abuser and spouse are similar. The mother, too overwhelmed by life's stresses, sees her child (usually a son) as someone to whom she can turn for nurture.

Whether the molester is father or mother, incestuous families demonstrate—

- an oversecretiveness in almost all their activities

- an overly possessive or restrictive attitude toward the daughter (especially on the father's part in father-daughter incest)

- blurred generational boundaries (generations do not have clear-cut roles—parents and children seem more like peers in their behavior)

- an atmosphere where siblings show marked jealousy toward one child who seems favored

- frequent opportunities for father and daughter to be alone.

Incestuous families guard their "secret" at all costs, often going to great lengths to preserve it.

There is another type of abuser whom some sources place in a separate category—the adolescent abuser. Adolescents are presented with numerous opportunities to molest children. Their role as babysitter is one prime chance. This is not to say that the number of trustworthy teenage babysitters does not far outweigh the potential abusers, but the opportunity exists for the latter nevertheless. Teenage boys are at the height of their sexual curiosity. Some may be experiencing too much conflict in their activities and may turn to children as a less demanding alternative.

A telling sign of a teenage boy who might be tempted to exploit children is a lack of contact with his peers. If the boy's willingness to help us with small children isn't *balanced* with an interest in peer activities and relationships, there might be reason to be concerned. (42, p. 91)

Older siblings may also be in a position to abuse much younger brothers and sisters.

The question often arises: "What is the difference between sexual exploration between agemates—considered a normal sideline of sexual awakening—and the sexual abuse of one minor by another?" One of the best rules of thumb relates to the level of power, knowledge, and resources each person has attained. In addition, most theorists agree that five years difference between the age of the older and the younger child in sexual interaction is usually the crucial difference (42, p. 90).

Whatever the particular symptoms the sexual abuser exhibits, the fact remains that the child suffers. An understanding of the behavior should, it is hoped, help teachers in their attempts to help the child.

The Emotionally Abusive Parent

The parent who emotionally abuses a child may have some of the same characteristics as the physically abusive or even the neglectful parent. The most obvious trait shared by all these individuals is an extremely poor self-image that manifests itself by striking out verbally as well as physically against someone closest to them—in this case, the child. Even more obviously than the other types of abusers, emotionally abusive parents come from all socioeconomic levels. Frequently, however, they too have been victims of childhoods that have prevented them from growing emotionally. Their family experiences—from life with a skid-row alcoholic to life with a wealthy public figure—may have been as different as their personalities.

Emotionally abusive parents include not only those who belittle, criticize, or even torture the child, but also those who fail to provide the support or affection that promote the child's healthy development. The latter condition is sometimes referred to as emotional neglect. Parents who have had little physical touching, affection, or encouragement from their own parents may have been deprived of a great deal of the emotional satisfaction that young children need. As a result of their own childhood experiences, they may neglect very vital needs of their own offspring—by not wanting the child, by being afraid of spoiling the child, by being reluctant to touch the child, or by not having time for the child.

In other words, emotionally neglectful parents may not comprehend the importance of reassurance, encouragement, and endearments to their offspring. If they do not feel comfortable about their own strengths and accomplishments, it will be difficult for them to recognize and acknowledge those of their child.

Emotionally abusive parents who are aggressive rather than neglectful in their acts are more difficult to understand, but perhaps they are more in need of understanding. These are individuals whose lives have taught them not to expect success, affection, and attention. Often they have a bitter attitude toward the hidden disappointments of the past. They may see the child as an extension of themselves, with the deficiencies painfully obvious. Or the child may be a symbol of a hated spouse, a parent perceived to be unfair or cruel, or an unfulfilled dream. Frequently, because of their own problems, these parents have little ability to realize the profound effect their criticisms, threats, or tortures may be having on the child. Therapy to improve their view of self may be the only way to help the child.

Whether the abuse or neglect is physical, emotional, or sexual, abusive and neglectful parents need help. They live in a world filled with pain and frustrations with which they have never learned to cope. The first step in helping such parents—and their children—is to see that their problems come to the attention of someone who can help them.

CHAPTER 9

How to Help the Child by Helping the Family

Understanding the Parents

Understanding the pathology involved in the abuse and neglect of children may on the one hand be helpful. On the other hand, no matter how great the intellectual understanding, when it comes to working with an abusive or neglectful parent, it may not be very easy to be the all-forgiving, all-knowing person one would wish to be. When a child has been hurt, concern for the child makes it difficult to forgive the adult who should have been capable of enough control or wisdom to protect the child. In the past, abusive parents were imprisoned for their misdeeds. History teaches, however, that one of the most effective ways to help the child is to understand and help the parent. An experienced high school teacher admitted the following reaction:

•

When I learned that Peggy was pregnant by her own father I was horrified. It was so against what I valued and believed in. I wondered what kind of monster could do this. When I first had to meet with Mr. C. I felt really ill. I conjured up retaliatory measures such as imprisonment for life or even castration. And yet when I finally met him I was stunned to realize who he was. Tom C.—that shy, unpopular boy I had attended high school with years before. I remembered the paintings he had done during art class—the pleading for understanding in his every look and brush stroke. After I was able to think of the misunderstood person beneath the outward appearance, I realized how I had looked at so many abusive and neglectful parents. Blinded by what they were doing to *my* students, I had not given myself a chance to realize that they were so thoroughly out of control of themselves and their lives, they were but children themselves.

•

Of course not all teachers have the advantage of knowing abusive parents before they come to the attention of society in such a despicable way. Nevertheless, it would be fairly safe to say that the problems of most of these parents are related to feelings of isolation that had their roots much earlier in their lives. Although their actions certainly cannot be condoned, the condemnation of society's intervention sends a message. Building their lives back to the point of being able to adequately care for their children—if this construction is possible—is a huge task, and to do this they need many helpers.

Helping the Parents

Although it is the role of the social service agency to treat the parents, the child's teacher can also be of great help. The suggestions that follow discuss some ways that teachers can aid parents—and indirectly the child.

1. Approach the parents in a noncondemnatory manner, no matter how you may be feeling. Indicating that you know how difficult it is for them to be in this situation may create a feeling that you are an ally. Try to assure the parents that you know that they love their child and want to do their best for the child in the future. Despite the apparent message of their actions, this is more than likely true.

Some parents have a very simplistic manner and may frustrate even the most well-meaning teacher. Extremely neglectful parents may need very simple explanations. Teachers who want these parents to help them with their children may need to go over their suggestions step by step. For example, "Help Johnny with his multiplication tables" may need to be spelled out: "When Johnny comes home, ask him for the cards I've given him here at school. Sit down with him and ask, '2 times 2 is what?' If he gives you the correct answer, put the card in one pile; if not, put the card in another pile and try the missed cards again later." Sometimes teachers assume that parents are not interested when they do not follow through with their requests. Remember, these parents may not lack motivation; they may lack understanding about what is expected of them.

In Chapter 7 I suggested that children may not understand the complex use of language or a series of commands given them in school because they lacked this exposure at home. It is easy to forget that the children's parents—especially those who are neglectful—may have had the same childhood experience themselves. Children learn to conceptualize at an early age with such elementary activities as seeing pictures in books and hearing or seeing the words to describe them. Adults guide them in these activities and speak to them with increasingly complex concepts as they mature. The assumption is, of course, that the adults in children's lives have achieved a level of conceptualization that goes beyond juvenile storybooks. Some parents, however, never mature in their language or their ability to conceptualize. In such cases, they are unable to help their children in this area (6).

Thus when you encounter a parent whose language development has not progressed beyond the most basic conceptualizations, the parent may appear either very limited or hostile. You may need to explain things carefully and ask for feedback about his or her comprehension. It is possible to do this in such a way that the parent will feel understood rather than demeaned.

2. Keep the parents up-to-date on the child's progress. Parents need to feel in control. They need to think that you and they are intent upon the same thing: the child's best interest. You may have to reach out to them and overlook, in your own mind, the frustration of initial rejection. If this rejection continues, all you can do is figuratively leave the door open for future communication.

3. Encourage parental involvement in school programs and activities—PTA, adult education, parenting programs, other parent groups. Remember that these parents have been isolated with little or no support and they need contact with peers. Some may not receive your suggestions with enthusiasm, but after your careful coaxing, sending meeting announcements home with the child, asking other parents to reach out, they may eventually respond. Other parents may welcome this new attention readily.

Adult education programs not only provide socialization, but they also teach skills that the abusive parent can use as an outlet. One abusive mother, for example, enrolled in a "Know Your Auto" course designed primarily to familiarize participants with the workings of a car, either to make minor repairs or to recognize possible trouble when consulting a mechanic. As a single parent, one of this woman's most stressful experiences centered around transportation and an aging car. Knowing her car helped her to feel more in control and thus freed her from one more stress.

In one school, a colleague and I led a *parent support group* created and sponsored by the school to assist parents in dealing with the everyday issues of parenting. Such an activity can be extremely helpful to the insecure parent. This group discussed ways to handle specific situations, invited speakers on a variety of child management topics, and generally provided support for participants in parenting endeavors. One of the more successful programs in dealing with abusive parents is Parents Anonymous, a support group specifically for such parents. (See Appendix E.)

Parenting skills workshops are another

method to strengthen parental confidence. Parent Awareness, for example, is a group learning experience designed to help parents explore positive alternatives in parenting. A series of workshops examines such important topics as explaining sexuality to children, positive methods of discipline, handling sibling issues, building a positive self-image and independence, dealing with children's fears, understanding child development, explaining death to a child, helping children adjust to divorce, and dealing with feelings in general. A comprehensive program such as this is worthwhile for all parents, but it is especially helpful to those who have difficulty coping. (See Appendix I.)

Courses in child development are useful too. The fact that some parents have too high expectations for their children points out the importance of such courses. Knowledge of child development should encourage more realistic parental expectations for children of various ages.

Other professionals within the school setting can also be helpful. Nurses can conduct health-related workshops or enlighten parents as to the types of testing available. Guidance personnel or others schooled in career development can provide counseling or workshops on job skill inventories. The list continues, stressing as much enhancement of parental potential as possible.

4. Above all, try to discern parental strengths and focus on them. Encourage parents in areas where you know they will meet with success. As a social worker, I used to try to discover at least one or two strengths whenever I met with abusive or neglectful clients. It was not always easy, but I found that it helped me to help them engineer their own successes.

Certainly teachers' conference time is limited. It is possible, however, to carry on excellent relationships with parents through notes. A friendly note praising a child's latest accomplishment, especially if taught by the parent, is enough to brighten the day of an otherwise isolated, overwrought caretaker.

5. *Know how your community can help.* If you do not know how to help the parents, consider finding out about local referral sources. For example, many communities have crisis hotlines for parents who cannot cope. (The local protective service agency or United Way or community services organization may have such a list.) Keep these telephone numbers available to give to the distraught parent.

Most of all, in working with abusive and neglectful parents, creativity is vital. Social services have not discovered all the answers in treatment. It could well be the support or a program offered by the local school system or its staff that makes the difference for the troubled parent, and thus for the maltreated child.

CHAPTER 10

Prevention: The Hope for the Future

In any discussion of prevention, the question emerges: "How do you find a good prevention program?" Prevention programs for the classroom must have certain characteristics. Teachers choosing materials should ask themselves several important questions.

Program Characteristics

1. Can the materials be integrated into the classroom curriculum?

A filmstrip or segment on prevention shown for a half hour during a year of study will seem artificial and staged. Prevention material can, however, be integrated into a variety of subjects. For example, younger classes could benefit from talking about feelings or perhaps writing about them in English or penmanship papers. Science classes could include segments on the body as a "marvelous machine" to help children recognize the importance of their bodies. The fact that their bodies are their own could be emphasized.

High school-age students could read *Oliver Twist* and use it to discuss the treatment of children in the past as well as in the present. Today, attempts are made to protect children from the kinds of abuse Oliver suffered.

Children of any age can be taught, at the level appropriate for them, that they as well as adults have basic human needs—for food, shelter, safety, and love and affection.

118

•

One creative teacher asked the children to cut out a multicolored pyramid (resembling Maslow's hierarchy of needs included in many psychology or organizational behavior texts) and to label each segment according to the level of needs represented. For example, at the bottom was the need to be physically comfortable. The children learned that if they were physically uncomfortable for some reason (such as hunger or fatigue), they had trouble doing less tangible things such as learning or creating.

•

As they begin to understand their own needs, children can realize where these needs are not being met consistently, and they may perhaps be able to ask for help.

Problem solving is a skill that could be integrated into many different lessons. Children learn problem-solving skills in simple math and algebra problems. Why not broaden these problems to include other life situations?

2. Is the prevention material I want to use appropriate to the age of the students?

As in every other type of learning, children need to presented with information that they are ready to absorb at their particular developmental level. For example, youngsters in the early grades can be taught about good and bad touch or how to express their feelings without calling it information that will protect them against sexual abuse. Giving children labels before they understand their meaning serves little purpose.

High schoolers may be ready to understand more about how people treat children. One high school English teacher used classics to explore society's view of children. The class then contrasted current materials in magazines, newspapers, and novels to see how attitudes toward children had changed.

3. Does the material reach children with different experiences in ways that will be meaningful to them?

Every classroom has children with a variety of experiences. Some have never been exposed to any behavior that could be considered abusive. Others may have been approached sexually, may have been exposed to careless parenting that is not quite neglectful, or may have been subject to severe discipline falling short of real harm to the child. Still others may previously have been or currently are victims of abuse or neglect. It is important that each child have the opportunity to receive something positive from the prevention materials used.

Some readings, lessons, or tapes, for example, imply that abuse (especially sexual abuse) is the worst thing a child can experience. Although adults may believe this, it is essential to remember that the kind of parenting or attention children have experienced in an abusive or neglectful situation is all they know. Children therefore feel that to condemn the abuser is to cut an important emotional lifeline. For a child who is currently being abused, such condemnation of an important figure in his or her life is unacceptable. Consequently, the child will accept the blame: "I must be bad—that's why Daddy has done this to me." Adults working with children should help them to recognize that the blame for hurting them is entirely the adult's, *but* give the youngsters the opportunity to recognize that adults are multifaceted. Although children have a right to be upset when the abuser exploits them, they may still care about that person.

Thus, children—especially those currently being abused—need help in recognizing that all persons—both adults and children—have rights and responsibilities. Children have the right not to be abused or exploited; they should let a trusted adult know if this happens to them.

Another concern for children who are currently being abused is the issue of saying no. Some materials present stories about children who have said no—especially in sexual abuse—and who have escaped the abuse. Youngsters who are being

120

abused need to know that just because they did not say no or because their no was overruled by the abuser, they are not weak or at fault. Adults have many ways of impressing their wishes on children. Their very size and strength (as well as the child's love for them) may be enough. Children must be helped to see that it is never too late to recognize that the adults in their lives are harming them. Telling another trusted adult should be stressed.

Children who have been approached sexually or who are the victims of severe parenting may also feel guilt or discomfort. A prevention program should emphasize that children should ask an adult if they are confused about what has happened to them.

•

A little girl came to a guidance counselor because she was confused about something that had happened to her. On a recent visit, an uncle had rubbed the child's upper leg in a way that had made her uncomfortable. The counselor helped the girl speak to her mother about it. The mother assured the child that she should say something if the uncle persisted. The girl's mother also promised to be conscious of the uncle's actions on the next visit. The child came away feeling protected as well as empowered to act on her own behalf.

•

Some parents who are asked to consider prevention programs for school worry that their children will be exposed to too much inappropriate information at too early an age. If a child is a victim of abuse or has been approached by an abuser, such knowledge may help the child recognize that he/she has been exploited and then tell an adult. Prevention materials can also help a child who has never been exposed to abuse or neglect—not only to recognize and resist possible future abusers, but in other ways as well.

4. Does the material encompass a variety of teachings that empower children to perform in numerous instances?

Preventive intervention in child abuse and neglect should be designed to guide children toward becoming healthy adults. Such growth requires many skills, both physical and emotional. Children must learn when they can and should do a task themselves, but they must also learn when to ask for help. A valuable component of a child abuse prevention program should be a section on whom and when to tell. It should consider fire, injury, being lost, and home emergencies, along with abduction, and being touched inappropriately by strangers or relatives. In an age of latchkey children, such information can be valuable to many youngsters.

5. Does the program elicit input from the children, encouraging them to try out what they are learning in a safe setting?

Everyone learns by doing, especially children. It is important that teachers present the material in a way that encourages responses. Children respond to incomplete stories that they can finish or by doing projects related to the material.

Child Abuse and Neglect: The NEA Multimedia Training Program includes a story tape for younger children called *A Dragon in My Closet.* The second side of the tape suggests ways that teachers can encourage discussion or assign projects. Young children seem to enjoy drawing Alfie (the imaginary dragon that becomes a confidant of an abused boy) as they listen to the tape. The story also provides a mechanism for discussions about feelings, death, trusting parents, problem drinking, and telling someone when one hurts. Children have acted out what they might have said to the boy if they were Alfie or a friend. One class made a collage of feelings—identifying those that could be expressed openly and those that would be difficult to tell others.*

---

*A similar tape for older students, *Deborah Wore Designer Jeans* (about sexual rather than physical abuse), is also included in *The NEA Multimedia Training Program.*

Older children might enjoy more extensive role play about feelings or dealing with friends who were abused. One class created a directory for children—especially useful for those who are alone while their parents work—to let them know the do's and don'ts of being alone and the numbers to call when they need help.

Whatever the particular learning experience, the child should be a participant.

6. Can the material be taught by a trusted adult—preferably the regular classroom teacher?

If prevention material is to be well integrated into the school program, it should be presented by someone with whom the child is familiar and whom the child trusts. Experts can help teachers become comfortable with and knowledgeable about the material, but the relationship of individual teachers with the students in their classes is a valuable part of the children's training.

Feeling comfortable in integrating prevention material may necessitate two things on your part. First, explore your own values and your comfort with the subject. Read several of the available books on abuse. In addition to providing valuable knowledge, some books are first person accounts of abuse. These may help you to recognize the need for early intervention.

Second, you may feel the need for more training yourself. Many schools are now appropriating money for in-service training for teachers. Insist on more than a brief one-session seminar. Your local protective agency or college may have someone who is skilled in training teachers. *Child Abuse and Neglect: The NEA Multimedia Training Program* (available from NEA, 1201 16th Street, NW, Washington, DC 20036) is a complete package designed to help teachers recognize and report abuse; it provides materials for prevention as well. There are also a variety of resources on the market. Search these out.

7. Does the material lend itself to repeated use throughout the grades—to help children integrate the information?

If a program is appropriate for the age of the children in a particular classroom, it may not be suitable for the following grades. Children need repetition and reinforcement of the materials at a more advanced level as they mature. Choose a program that covers several grades. Such a program, but one directed specifically toward sexual abuse, is the *Personal Safety Curriculum* (available through Geri Crisci, P.O. Box 763, Hadley, MA 01035).

Although designed for presentation in related segments, the material could be spread out during the course of a school year. The following year the information is to be repeated with slightly different emphases. For young children, the program recommends the film *Who Do You Tell?* (see Appendix I), a discussion of the resources children have to seek help in a number of situations. For older children, the same ideas are presented in a manner appropriate for their age level. Used through grades K–12, the program would provide students with improved self-concept, a knowledge of important resources, the skills to seek out trusted adults, and the ability to recognize and resist sexual abuse. Programs such as this could be used for the whole spectrum of abuse and neglect with thoughtful additions.

8. Does the material prepare children to be healthier adults?

The Introduction discussed the importance of preparing children for adult tasks. Not only should they learn to cope with the stress that is everywhere in modern life, but they also should be helped to assume (if they choose to do so) the most important role of adulthood—parenting. While people are trained for most other jobs, society assumes that when the first child is born, miraculously the parent will know how to be successful in parenting. So thoroughly does this attitude permeate our culture that many young parents are afraid to admit their ignorance.

It is my opinion that every high school student's program should include a course in parenting skills as well as one in human development. The former would guide would-be parents in assuming their future roles, while the latter would help them recognize what can be expected of children at any particular age. Since the problem for many abusive parents is unrealistic expectations, knowing what to expect could prevent later abusive behavior. These courses should use exercises to help students try on the role of parent. A particularly effective example is the "egg exercise." Students are given an egg, which they treat like a baby. It must be kept safe from harm, not left alone without a sitter, and generally treated with care. Students are often surprised at the amount of attention this requires and they are able to recognize how difficult parenting can be.

Another important task is to ensure that these future adults have learned the five lessons discussed in Chapter 8. If abusive parents have not learned how to make decisions, how to delay gratification, how to express their needs appropriately, how to take responsibility for their own actions, and how to tell the difference between feelings and actions, then students, by learning these emotional tasks, can be prepared to escape the profile of an abusing adult.

9. Can the program be connected to the community so that the learning is reinforced in other places?

Obtaining community support for a program to prevent sexual abuse may be difficult. But enlisting the support of parents and community leaders to emphasize the training of well-rounded adults may be easier. Has your school ever considered setting up a children's council to serve as a resource for the activities provided for children in your area? Such a group could also provide information to help Scouts, boys' and girls' clubs, Campfire Girls, and other youth groups integrate important concepts in their activities. Many organizations have already done so.

Chapter 9 discussed parenting skills workshops and parent support groups. Parents may also respond to workshops on issues of community concerns. For example, in one community where a rash of teen suicides had caused great anxiety, the school sponsored programs on "Adolescent Suicide." As prevention intervention, parents were encouraged to become more aware of their children's feelings and to communicate more openly. At the same time, high school students were discussing the subject in school. Because of the facilitated communication between students and their parents, the parents wholeheartedly supported the school's efforts.

Another school enlisted the support of a community service organization to buy prevention training materials as a service project. Such groups are often glad to support the school's efforts if they receive specific information about what materials are needed and where they can be obtained.

How to Find Materials to Use

There are many resources available (especially those related to child sexual abuse) that are designed for use by parents and teachers. Appendices I and J list numerous sources and publishers and information on how to obtain these materials. Organizations dedicated to protective services or to preventing child abuse may also be helpful. Consider writing to offices such as the National Committee for Prevention of Child Abuse, the National Center on Child Abuse and Neglect, the National Center for Missing and Exploited Children, and ACTION for Child Protection for listings of their materials (see Appendix E for addresses). Be sure to specify your exact needs using the criteria previously suggested in this chapter.

In addition to these organizations, there are clearinghouses that carry a variety of materials on child abuse for children and adults. One such group, *KIDSRIGHTS* (see Appendix J), features child abuse literature, but it also offers publications and tapes on other aspects of "Kidsrights" that are of concern to parents and teachers. Catalogs of such groups may be useful tools for choosing appropriate books or programs.

Once you have ideas about materials to use, consider them in the light of the previously mentioned criteria. Some resources may be excellent, but do not fit your needs. Can they be adapted for use? Some ingenuity on your part may be required, but joining with other teachers in the school may help. For example, two teachers in the Clinton (Massachusetts) school system obtained a grant for training their colleagues and integrating prevention materials into the school system. Then they designed a ten-week course for teachers to learn how to detect, report, and prevent child abuse. Experts were called in for particular sessions, including the last few when teachers were taught how to use the information in their classrooms. The school system then collected resources from a number of places to be housed in the school library. Now teachers not only have ideas about integrating materials in their classroom, but they also have a selection of books, filmstrips, and exercises they can use.

In Worcester (Massachusetts), the schools undertook a citywide sexual abuse prevention program. They made use of an interagency team to provide resources. A full description of this effort is included in Appendix B.

However you accomplish the task, classroom teachers have many opportunities—if not a duty—to educate children in the prevention of abuse and neglect. After all, prevention *is* the hope for the future.

Checklist for Choosing
an Effective Prevention Program

	Yes	No

Does the program or material—

1. lend itself to integration into regular class-room materials? ____ ____

   How? _____

   Can it be modified? ____ ____

2. lend itself to the age of my students? ____ ____

   Can it be modified? ____ ____

   How? _____

3. reach children with different experience? ____ ____

   Those who are abused? ____ ____

   Those who have been exposed to abuse? ____ ____

   Those who have not been abused? ____ ____

4. encompass learnings to empower children in numerous instances? ____ ____

   Can it be modified? ____ ____

   How? _____

5. get children involved in their learning? ____ ____

   List the exercises

   _____

   _____

   _____

   Can it be modified to include more? ____ ____

   How? _____

6. seem comfortable for me to teach? ____ ____

   What do I need to become more comfortable doing so?

   _____

	Yes	*No*

Reading materials? (List)

_____

_____

_____

More training? (Do I have a plan for getting it?)

_____

7. lend itself to being repeated in other years?   _____   _____

   How can it be modified?

   _____

8. prepare children for a number of adult tasks?   _____   _____

   Examples:

   Problem solving   _____   _____

   Concerns of parenting   _____   _____

   Human development   _____   _____

   Stress reduction   _____   _____

   Asking for help   _____   _____

   Self-reliance   _____   _____

   Other

   _____

   _____

   _____

9. lend itself to integration in community programs?   _____   _____

   Does the material include or can it be modified to include information on

   Body awareness?   _____   _____

   Rights and responsibilities?   _____   _____

   Saying no?   _____   _____

	Yes	No
Asking for help?	___	___
Knowing whom to ask for help?	___	___
Recognizing feelings?	___	___
Expressing feelings?	___	___
Making decisions?	___	___
Separating feelings and behavior?	___	___
Taking responsibility for one's actions?	___	___
Handling anger?	___	___
Feeling good about oneself?	___	___

No one program will meet all these criteria. Careful choices of existing materials, however, will enable you to create your own program—the one that is best for you.

CHAPTER 11

Prevention: Concerns and Evaluation

Because of the critical need for extensive preventive education in our nation's schools, I want to draw special attention to certain areas not fully developed elsewhere in this publication. These areas are children's developmental stages, multicultural concerns, and prevention program evaluation. The following selections discuss these concerns: "Considering Children's Developmental Stages in Prevention Education" by Caren Adams, "Child Sexual Abuse Prevention Project in an Hispanic Community" by Geraldine A. Crisci and Maria Idali Torres, "Harmful Effects of School-based Sexual Abuse Prevention Programs? Reassure the Parents" by Sandy K. Wurtele and Cindy L. Miller-Perrin, and "How Programs Are Evaluated" by Ellen Gray and Joan Di Leonardi.

Considering Children's Developmental Stages in Prevention Education*

Caren Adams

Sexual abuse prevention education began in response to requests for adult rape prevention information. Parents wanted to know what to say to their children that could help protect them. By looking at how sexual abuse often begins and who the offenders are, some general statements were developed to guide parents in talking with their children. It was

---

*Reprinted with permission from *The Educator's Guide to Preventing Child Sexual Abuse*, Network Publications, a division of ETR Associates (1986), Santa Cruz, CA.

assumed parents would tailor what they said to their particular children, depending on their developmental stage and readiness.

With increasing concern about sexual abuse and the desire to reach all children came the expansion of these general premises into curriculum, often for presentation in schools. When the information is designed with consideration for the developmental stage of children, it is usually done by giving younger children less information about the sexual nature of abuse, and sometimes with the use of age-appropriate materials such as coloring books, dolls or puppets.

Despite such program adjustments, children may be exposed to information that is not developmentally appropriate. Thus it is time to reexamine prevention premises in light of child development and reconsider what children are being taught in school programs. What works for parents because they can monitor their child and help her or him understand through repetition and modeling, may not be as appropriate in a school setting.

The four basic concepts of sexual abuse prevention education are discussed below.

1. Children need to know enough about what sexual abuse is to recognize it if it happens or begins to happen. Children may need information about who an offender might be, what force (such as trickery, secrets or bribery) might be used, some description of specific abusive behaviors, and perhaps a possible answer as to why some people abuse children. The definition of sexual abuse has often been reduced to "someone touching your private parts," or "when children get forced or tricked into touch/sexual contact." The concept of good, bad and confusing touch has been used as a way to explain abuse without always having to use sexual vocabulary.

2. Children need to know they have the right to say no or resist in some other way. The levels of resistance suggested include getting away, saying no, and resisting physically.

3. Children need to tell someone if they are uncomfortable or unsure of a situation.

4. Children need to know it isn't their fault if abuse happens.

These concepts are logical and are based on what is known about how sexual abuse occurs. They are not necessarily based adequately on knowledge of what makes sense to children at different ages. When parents are the educators, they can be the judge of what is appropriate. Although parents often underestimate their child's ability to understand and cope if the subject is explained honestly, they can avoid some of the mistakes of the more general classroom presentation.

132

Programs often spend a great deal of time teaching children how to react, say no and/or use physical self-defense. But they may spend little time identifying what sexual abuse actually is. The definition is usually vague and/or describes only one form of sexual abuse. Because of the fear of prevention education being perceived as sex education, most programs have avoided defining abuse in sexual terms, and have preferred instead to talk about touch or private parts. The unfortunate consequence is that touch appears to be the problem. It is also misleading in that abuse may begin with requests to undress or look at an adult who is undressed, rather than with touching.

Children often make assumptions when they are given simple generalizations, such as no one has the right to touch your private parts. Some children have decided a beloved caretaker shouldn't wash them. Others have concluded they should not touch themselves. Thus, the issue of touching needs much more attention in developmental terms. What generalizations can children make about sexual abuse? How specific is it necessary to be? The more specific the information, the more time must be spent and resources developed covering each aspect.

Although prevention programs make efforts to include the benefits of good touch, the emphasis is on refusing bad or confusing touch. Cordelia Anderson's original concept encouraged children to talk about different kinds of touch, and in so doing, encouraged children to accept good touch. But the message is sometimes so diluted when it is shortened and retranslated in the process of curriculum development, that sexual abuse prevention appears to be antitouch.

Most programs sidestep the specific identification of possible offenders because they don't want to be accused of making children suspicious or of betraying family trust. Educators usually deal with the issue by saying "if someone you know touches you . . ." Unfortunately most children, even older children, do not have the ability to translate this generalization to mean father, grandfather, Uncle John, cousin Carol or the babysitter. Furthermore, including avoidance of abduction within the safety curriculum leads children to consider anyone a stranger.

Prevention programs present different strategies to help children avoid victimization. Children should tell, say no, get away, follow the rules, have a safety plan, and/or learn a self-defense yell. Although these are good ideas, the ability of children of different ages to understand and use these strategies needs to be examined. Above all, the idea that children *should* respond in a certain way must be avoided. Children have the right to grow up free of unwanted sexual contact. That they don't does not mean they are obligated to know how to respond. Children may be getting the message that sexual abuse is their fault if they don't know how to stop it. This is exactly the opposite of what is intended. Prevention educators want children to know that it is not their fault no matter what they did or didn't do. But they are working against the moral development of children who believe if an adult does something, it must be right. So if it was wrong, the children must be at fault.

Simply telling children otherwise is not sufficient if other prevention activities carry the message that children are responsibile for protecting themselves. Self-protection strategies should be viewed as optional skills for children to have. Adults should be protecting children by not preying on them and by being alert for signs that others are.

Developmental Issues and Conflicts

For preschoolers, no one is a stranger after the first hello. Thus, some programs attempt to teach the difference between acquaintances and strangers. Given the fact that 85 percent of children are abused by someone they know, the need to help children make this distinction may not be a high priority.

Children under the age of six are especially afraid of monsters, ghosts and other imaginary figures. They may frighten easily at the idea that yet another danger is out there somewhere. Their fear may be compounded by the fact that young children use small details and examples to try to make sense of generalizations. If the man in the film is wearing a red shirt, they may decide that all men wearing red shirts are bad.

Asking young children to say no to adult authority seems unfair. Children need to be able to trust adults and feel secure in their care. The notion that adults can be untrustworthy and may hurt children is disturbing and potentially frightening. Children will either ignore the message or blame themselves. Prevention programs need to balance their approach with more statements that the majority of adults would not hurt them in any way.

The message that no one has the right to touch your private parts should be reevaluated for preschoolers. While preschoolers can be taught self-care as part of their move toward independence, many circumstances—including hygiene, medical care and first aid—legitimately require a caretaker's touch.

Prevention programs need to carefully evaluate the messages they are conveying about parents and other caretakers. Sexual abuse is serious and many more children are vulnerable than the public believes. However, when considering the balance between making children aware and undermining their trust in adults, it is important to remember that many children will not be sexually abused, and many more children will not be sexually abused by a parent or parent figure. There are many who doubt that abuse by trusted authority figures can be prevented by programs for young children because they simply don't have the power to resist.

Children in kindergarten through second grade are still likely to view adults as godlike. Although this age group is in the process of changing, they still believe adults are right, and continue to believe if something bad happens to them, it must have been their fault. They may also focus on wrongdoing they understand (such as telling lies or breaking rules) rather than the sexual abuse. They also may be concerned about being a tattletale. Boys of this age and older are convinced of their ability to use super heroic force to get out of any situation. Their need to be tough and strong may not allow them to see any of the sexual abuse prevention information as relevant to them.

Children in third through sixth grades are moving toward making independent judgments about people's behavior and the consequences of breaking rules. By fifth and sixth grades, children display great diversity in development. Some children, mostly girls, are maturing physically and encountering pressure for sexual contact from older boys. Children of this age will readily agree that adults make mistakes and can be wrong. Unfortunately they may not see adults as helpful with the problems they face. They may resent being treated like little children or they may be embarrassed.

For children in junior high, an important developmental shift is occurring. They are beginning or continuing an interest in opposite sex relationships. They may begin dating. Some are already involved in sexual intercourse. Assault by peers of older teens becomes part of the gamut of sexual abuse. But talk about touching private parts or confusing touch isn't necessarily helpful in identifying an abusive situation. Most touch at this age is confusing and ambiguous in its meaning. Adolescents beginning to experiment with kissing, hugging and other sexual interactions are unlikely to tell an adult about puzzling or confusing touch. Often they are most interested in knowing: Does this mean he likes me? How far can I get her to go? And even abusive, exploitative touch or sexual interaction may seem preferable to a teen than nothing.

By junior high, young teens are under enormous pressure. They are uncertain of who they are and what values they hold. They are trying to break free of parental restrictions. It is a time of extreme vulnerability; a time when they need information about relationships and sexuality. But their overriding need to be cool, sophisticated and appear knowledgeable about sex often prevents them from asking the questions about confusing or abusive touch they might like to. They must be given specific permission to ask those questions. They are rarely reached by prevention programs, which too often are simply an extension of younger children's programs. Besides, sexual abuse prevention for teens means addressing sexual issues, and prevention programs have been reluctant to do so.

The transition in ability to reason abstractly begins as teens enter high school, but junior high students still need concrete examples and suggestions.

Young people in high school consider themselves to be independent and competent. This belief may be so strong teenagers won't ask for protection even when they realize they may need it. They want to be able to handle situations on their own and not feel like babies who need their parents' help. They are ready for information about how an offender might behave.

Teens, unlike younger children, are less likely to make black and white distinctions between people. They react negatively to anything that feels like an attack on peers and to anything that sounds antimale. Teens are at a develpmental stage in which they are taking risks rather than being careful. They may be more concerned about being liked than in resisting abuse.

Recommendations and Modifications

1. Prevention programs for preschoolers should recognize the potential for frightening children and/or overgeneralizing. Preschoolers should only be taught to tell an adult if they don't understand why someone is touching them. Programs to help them gain the vocabulary to tell if they are abused and to label their feelings are probably most consistent with other learning going on at this time.

The major prevention effort for this age child should be directed toward their parents. Parents need to know the indicators of abuse and how to respond. And preschoolers must be told they can tell their parents if they need help. Even though some parents are offenders, most will help their children if they have adequate information and resources.

136

2. The original goal of prevention was to give children enough information to be able to respond to a sexual abuse situation before it became serious, not to make them responsible for protecting themselves. That distinction needs to be reaffirmed and strengthened. We want children to know enough to react, not to feel responsible if they are unable to respond.

3. The importance of parents, especially to elementary age children, needs to be incorporated more fully into prevention programs.

4. Programs for teens should address more adequately the complex issues of relationship interactions, abusive behavior in general and values about coercive behavior. Educators should recognize the adolescents' need to be competent and independent.

Child Sexual Abuse Prevention Project in an Hispanic Community*

Geraldine A. Crisci
Maria Idali Torres

The project described below originated as one of six model demonstration projects funded by the National Center on Child Abuse and Neglect in October, 1980. This project entitled Child Sexual Abuse: Education and Prevention Among Rural and Hispanic Children, focused on a rural, Anglo site and an urban, Hispanic site. Both sites are situated in western Massachusetts. The rationale for site selection was a concern for making prevention information accessible to populations having the least access to services.

The project used a train-the-trainer model. Staff trained teachers at both sites to work directly with children. The target populations were children from preschool through sixth grade. In addition to a classroom curriculum guide, resources included the puppet production, *What Should I Do?* and the film, *Who Do You Tell?* This project reached the largest number on non-Anglo children and was the only one attempting extensive work with preschoolers.

The purpose of all six projects was to in-

*Reprinted with permission from *The Educator's Guide to Preventing Child Sexual Abuse*, Network Publications, a division of ETR Associates (1986), Santa Cruz, CA.

crease knowledge and awareness of child sexual abuse through the development and implementation of educational strategies. Questions initially posed included the following. Can child sexual abuse be prevented? If so, can educational materials be developed for use with children and families? Can such materials be evaluated as having an impact on the problem? Can programs gain access to schools and communities? This last question was perhaps the most critical. The finest educational materials have limited value if they do not reach children and their families.

Gaining access to the target population is primary. The approach used by this project was based on a public health model of prevention and a mental health model of community needs assessment.

Site Description

The Massachusetts Migrant Education Program (MMEP) was the formal site for our work with the Hispanic community. MMEP is a federally funded supplemental education program for the children of migrant farm workers. The MMEP provides an eight-week summer program, operating five days a week, 8:30-3:00, for children preschool through grade 12. Children participating in the summer program attend public school during the academic year and live, for the most part, with their families in the urban areas of Springfield, Holyoke and Chicopee. The MMEP provides supplemental education in reading, math and language skills as well as offering physical education, art and theater. Paid staff include bilingual and bicultural teachers, teacher aides and parent aides who work in teams in the classroom.

Parent involvement is achieved through large parent meetings held at the beginning and end of the summer, various special parent training workshops and events held throughout the summer, and the unique classroom parent-aide program. The parent aides work daily with the children. Their involvement enriches the classroom environment culturally and provides skill training and part-time jobs for participating parents.

The population served is 97 percent Puerto Rican, 1 percent Black, 1 percent Portuguese, and 1 percent Anglo. This project was given a unique opportunity to work with Puerto Rican children and their families in a formal educational setting. The structure of the MMEP and its many services (including transportation for children and parents) provided an almost ideal environment in which to develop the Hispanic component of a prevention program.

138

Prevention and Community Assessment Model

This project followed a public health model of prevention and used both formal and informal assessment methods in each stage of the work. This point cannot be emphasized enough. Project descriptions and conceptualizations often look great on paper, yet fail in their attempt at implementation. A clear assessment process that follows the three stages of project development and completion—planning, implementation and evaluation—is a critical factor in the success of a prevention program.

This process becomes especially important when working with a community whose culture is not Anglo. Additionally, the sensitive (and often confusing) issue of child sexual abuse prevention heightens the necessity of careful planning and community preparation that allows for direct input and feedback from representative members of the community. In this project, parents, children, community spokespeople and teaching staff were defined as representative members.

Public Health Model of Prevention

Prevention is defined as efforts made to reduce the incidence and prevalence of the problem. There are three levels of prevention in this model: primary, secondary and tertiary. Primary prevention efforts are aimed at the general population and geared toward providing education and training in health and skill enhancement. At this level it is sometimes possible to identify high risk groups or detect the initial stage of a problem. There are secondary gains; however, the focus remains general and educative.

At the secondary level of prevention, efforts are aimed at those persons who are already in a problem situation and who may have a short history of abuse, or who live in abusive families. All efforts are geared to a group already identified as having a problem and requiring specific clinical intervention.

At the tertiary level of prevention, the effort is clinical intervention with a population having a long history or chronic problems. Again, the population and intervention are specific.

This project is a primary prevention effort based on the belief that education is the most effective method of prevention. Through the development of creative problem-solving skills and understanding and use of social support systems, children can attain the life skills needed to prevent sexual abuse and to insure safety in their lives. The best educational strategies develop skills transferable to other life situations, especially in the identification of potentially dangerous situations.

Needs Assessment

During the planning stage, meetings with parents, teachers, social service providers and community liaisons provided an informal needs assessment. At these meetings staff explained the project and conducted an awareness training on child sexual abuse. This awareness training has proven to be one of the most successful components. It provides a way to inform participants about the extent of the problem, its definition and dynamics, and most of all, to engender empathy for sexually victimized children. The goal is to facilitate an understanding of the necessity for prevention programs and to form an alliance with participants in working toward implementation. Awareness is essential. People cannot support prevention unless they understand the need. Most parents are not aware of the risks to their children and many think that "stranger danger" is the greatest risk. Therefore they only provide their children with warnings about kidnapping.

At the conclusion of the meeting participants were asked to voice their concerns, identify potential problems, make suggestions for teaching, and define their individual roles in prevention efforts. Participants were also asked to work with project staff, preferably taking a leadership role in helping us learn community norms and understand priorities, problems (for instance with the formal support system) and concerns. Community leaders and groups were informed about the project and included in the assessment as well.

Curriculum Concepts and Goals

The classroom curriculum is built on four major concepts believed to be the building blocks of sexual abuse prevention education: support systems (formal and informal), privacy, the touch continuum (developed by Cordelia Anderson) and assertiveness. The goals are to help children: (1) learn and understand the touch continuum, (2) be able to use their instincts in differentiating between exploitative and nurturant touch, (3) know that support systems exist for them (families, friends, neighbors, schools and community), (4) be able to identify the support systems that will be most useful to them in any given situation, (5) learn to use various community resources, (6) know ways to avoid and resist unsafe situations, (7) learn to use problem-solving skills to generate alternatives in potentially dangerous situations and (8) learn assertiveness skills.

Clearly these concepts are value-laden; families differ in their beliefs about privacy and touch. Further, teaching children to use support systems and assertiveness in their relationships with adults may be potentially threatening to a family's authority figures. The curriculum, titled the *Personal Safety Curriculum,* is taught within the context of body safety and protection from potentially dangerous situations through early identification. It is important for parents to have the opportunity to understand this context and use the concepts at home. Thus parent involvement is a key component and understanding cultural values is critical to successful implementation. We will share our findings through a discussion of the four concepts looking at cultural implications with a focus on the Hispanic community.

Support Systems

Who can you tell if you are in a potentially dangerous situation? The concept of family is a strong value within Puerto Rican culture. It has been our experience, however, that a typical Puerto Rican family is a myth. Great diversity exists among Puerto Rican families.

Nonetheless, the family is seen as the main source of support. The concept of extended family is a belief that is held to be true whether or not, in practice, an extended family exists. Parents tried to teach this concept, but their children did not easily relate to it, given few role models and the emphasis on the nuclear family in school. Many of the families who participated in the project, in fact, fell into the transitional family structure between extended and nuclear.

Two other sets of information proved helpful in understanding how to teach the concept of support systems. The first is an awareness of the cultural differences between Anglo and Puerto Rican families. (See Figure 1.)

Differences vary according to level of acculturation. The second is an understanding of help-seeking preferences. Our observations that Puerto Rican families follow a 3-step process are similar to those of Sonia Badillo-Ghali and Melvin Belgado. (See Figure 2.)

Human service agencies are often perceived by the Hispanic community as being inaccessible. Often they use the services only for economic reasons.

Cultural Differences Between Anglo and Puerto Rican Families

Concepts	Anglo	Puerto Rican
Language	Monolingual	Bilingual
Culture	Monocultural	Bicultural
Age	Segregation	Integration
	Children have their own activities	Children must spend time with the family
	Adolescents geared toward peers	Adolescents geared toward elders
Attitudes	Assertiveness	Nonassertiveness
	Egocentric: own needs first	Other-oriented: other's needs first

Figure 1

Help-Seeking Preferences of Puerto Rican Families

1	2	3
family	teachers	community agencies
relatives	clergy	
friends	educated people	
neighbors	(within social	
acquaintances	service network)	
shopkeepers	bilingual/bicultural	
	people working in	
	social services	

Figure 2

The concept of family is emphasized in the curriculum. But children are also taught that sometimes their family may not be available, or may not understand the problem and how to solve it. This necessitates the need for children to know what is offered in the community.

In assessing cultural factors in teaching this concept we looked at the language, beliefs, attitudes, practices and values of the community. Information about each of these factors was gained through our informal assessment process. Other factors considered in our assessment were: age of parents, number of years child and family had lived in the United States (this may differ among siblings and between parents and children), family structure, bilingualness, genera-

142

tional picture and demographics. All of these factors were further assessed within the context of the American culture (given that children were being socialized within the public school systems) with two major influences requiring special consideration: traditional culture and socioeconomic class.

Failure to understand and integrate this information about Puerto Rican families considerably limits intervention efforts. The major questions are: Who are the families in the community? Do they need prevention education?

Some considerations we found helpful in assessing the Puerto Rican family included: number of years in the United States, level of acculturation, rural vs. urban background, age of parents and age of children.

Privacy

Two factors required consideration in teaching the concepts of the right to privacy in general and the right to body privacy as well. First, Puerto Ricans are family oriented and believe personal problems are family problems. The positive aspect of their belief is that the family is willing to be supportive with personal problems. The negative aspect is that if the problem is caused by a family member, the child may not want the rest of the family to know.

Secondly, Puerto Rican family members express a willingness to accommodate the needs of others, which are considered more important than one's own needs. This can mean individuals have no private space or private conversations. We approached the privacy concept directly through a discussion of private body parts. This direct educational effort was more comfortable for parents who reported teaching children body privacy from an early age. (Note: This was in direct contrast with our work in the rural, Anglo site where parents felt the abstract concepts should be taught prior to body privacy concepts.)

Touch Continuum

Physical affection and expressed warmth for children was a cultural value and norm in the communities in which we worked. Teaching the touch continuum to children was viewed as positive and helpful. There is a very clear understanding of the differences between nurturance and exploitation on the part of Puerto Rican parents. (Note: This seemed a more complex issue at other sites.)

Assertiveness

The goal of this concept is to teach the right to say no to an unwanted touch. This was a foreign concept within the Puerto Rican culture and required considerable discussion between staff, parents and teachers to find acceptable ways of teaching this skill. (This concept has required the most work with parents across sites.) In the Puerto Rican families the major concern was that children not lose respect for parents. Clearly, teaching assertiveness conflicts with their cultural norms. Puerto Rican children are taught not to look directly at adults when speaking to them; direct eye contact is an assertive body language posture. Cultural expectations of children are that they be obedient and meet other people's needs. Saying no and meeting one's own needs (for safety) may be in conflict with meeting someone else's needs.

Even though the concept was in conflict with cultural norms, mothers supported the idea of teaching assertiveness skills and participated in assertiveness workshops arranged by project staff. We found that responding to requests for more adult training assisted in the problem-solving process around cultural-norm conflicts. Initiative for the problem solving was taken by the parents.

Implementation

A formal process for assessing the implementation of the program was conducted in the following manner:

1. Project staff and teaching staff draft curriculum activities

2. Activities presented to parents

3. Parent feedback incorporated into activities

4. Activity presented in the classroom by teacher, teacher aide and parent aide

5. Results and observations of the presented activity shared with parents

6. Activity again presented in classroom (with revision if necessary)

7. Activity again presented to parents

Parents reviewing the curriculum activities met weekly for 90 minutes. Through this process the cultural appropriateness of activities was evaluated. Our goal was to produce bicultural as well as bilingual curriculum materials.

Evaluation

Young children (ages 3 to 7) who participated in the preschool and elementary school program were interviewed to determine their comprehension of the topics covered. The critical question was whether children of these ages have the cognitive ability to understand the concepts. One colloquial assumption about child sexual abuse prevention is that the information is too complex or too scary to be presented to younger children. Our results indicate that even young children were able to grasp the basic information of a personal safety program.

The *Personal Safety Curriculum* was taught during the eight-week summer program of the MMEP to children from preschool through grade five. However, only preschool through second grades were included in this study. The children received weekly lessons from the *Personal Safety Curriculum*, each lesson ranging from 15 to 50 minutes in length. Posters and coloring sheets from the lessons were posted in the classrooms throughout the summer sessions. Children in the first and second grades also saw the film, *Who Do You Tell?* Children in preschool through second grade saw the puppet show, *What Should I Do?*

Since children ages 3 to 7 have no or limited reading and writing ability, the testing was conducted by interview. Children were shown pictures from the book *Red Flag/Green Flag People* and from the *Touch* educational materials developed by Illusion Theater. All children were shown two good touch pictures and two bad touch pictures, and asked questions concerning the concepts illustrated.

The study was conducted during the last 10 to 14 days of the summer program. All interviews were conducted at the MMEP site by the Project Educator who was bilingual. Children were asked the questions in both Spanish and English, and responded in whichever language they wished. Younger children tended to use Spanish and older children English.

The most striking result was that even young children were able to comprehend the curriculum, which concentrated on the concepts of good and bad touch and telling someone. Only first and second grade children were asked the question about privacy, but seven of the eight groups indicated an understanding of the concept. The overall percentage correct was 70 percent for preschool, 75 percent for kindergarten, 80 percent for first grade, and 85 percent for second grade. The statistics are even more impressive for the preschool and kindergarten children who were interviewed individually. The first and second grade children were interviewed in groups, which would tend for them to have higher scores.

The children's verbal responses to all questions were recorded during the interviews for a purpose other than evaluation. The words and phrases the children used to convey their ideas served as a resource list for the final translation of the *Personal Safety Curriculum* into Spanish.

References

Badillo-Ghali, Sonia. "Cultural Sensitivity in the Puerto Rican Client." *Social Casework* (October 1977).

Badillo-Ghali, Sonia. "Understanding Puerto Rican Traditions." *Social Work* 27:1 (1982).

Belgado, Melvin and Denise Humm-Belgado. "Natural Support Systems as a Source of Strength in the Puerto Rican Community." *Social Work* 27:1 (1982).

Harmful Effects of School-based Sexual Abuse Prevention Programs? Reassure the Parents*

Sandy K. Wurtele
Cindy L. Miller-Perrin

Although the 1980 Gallup Poll indicated that 80 percent of U.S. adults were in favor of having sex education taught in the schools, less than 10 percent of the students in this country actually receive such instruction (Kirby, Alter, and Scales, 1979). Several barriers in implementing such programs may account for the discrepancy between public opinion and school policy. Scales and Kirby (1983) found that the single greatest barrier to implementing sex education programs was administrators' fear of community opposition. Other problems noted by researchers have included: (a) differences between parents', students', teachers' and administrators' goals and expectations for sex education (e.g., Dearth, 1974; Hale and Gustavus, 1978); (b) teachers' concerns that they have not been sufficiently trained to deal with the sensitive subject of human sexuality (Munson, 1976; Ryan and Dunn, 1979); (c) parents' concerns regarding usurpation of their rights and their fears

*Paper presented at the meeting of the 94th Annual Convention of the American Psychological Association, Washington, D.C., August 1986. Reprinted with permission of the authors.

that such programs may result in sexual experimentation (Cook, 1972); and (d) the fear that learning about sexuality will be harmful to children and adolescents (Brown, 1981).

With all the controversy over teaching sex education in the schools, it is no wonder that teachers, administrators, and parents have reservations about dealing with a related topic: child sexual abuse. The sexual abuse of children occurs at an alarming rate. The National Incidence Study estimates an annual rate of 0.7 cases of child sexual abuse per 1,000 children (DHHS, 1981). Further evidence for the frequency of this abuse comes from retrospective studies of adults. In one survey, as many as one of every four women and one of every eleven men reported experiencing some form of sexual abuse or molestation during their childhood (Finkelhor, 1979). Certainly the need is great for programs aimed at preventing the sexual abuse of children.

While the necessity for such programs seems to be relatively obvious in light of the numerous children abused and the magnitude of the ramifications of that abuse (Gelinas, 1983; Mrazek and Mrazek, 1981), child sexual abuse prevention programs are still not being implemented in all schools. There appear to be three major reasons why school systems may be reluctant to address this need. First, teachers have been noted to have several concerns regarding the area of sexual abuse and reservations about educating children on this topic (Hazzard, 1984). For example, Lynch (1975) reported that many teachers were afraid of parental reprisal after a report of abuse; some were hesitant to become involved in the legal system. McCaffrey and Tewey (1978) observed that teachers often felt uncomfortable talking with children or parents about abuse-related issues and frequently expressed confusion about how to work with protective service agencies. In addition, Pelcovitz (1978) reported that some teachers felt unsupported by principals in dealing with abuse cases. With regard to educating children about sexual abuse, many teachers appear to lack knowledge about important aspects of child abuse (Hazzard, 1984). This knowledge deficit may be due to lack of training in child abuse identification and intervention. Surveys of colleges offering degrees in education have found that only about two-thirds of the education programs include information on child abuse in the regular curriculum (e.g., Bartlett, 1978). In addition, the quality of this training was questioned by the Education Commission of the states (1978).

The other two reasons for our school systems' reluctance to effectively educate children about sexual abuse appear to be administrators' concerns and parents' fears regarding the consequences of such programs. Many administrators fear community disapproval, and many parents express concern about the harmful effects of such programs. For

147

example, parents are sometimes afraid that if their children participate in a sexual abuse prevention program, they may be frightened of strangers, be uncomfortable accepting their parents' physical displays of affection, suffer from nightmares, etc. While these fears have been expressed to us on an informal basis and have served as barriers for implementing prevention programs, we are not aware of any research aimed at determining the actual extent of such negative side effects of school-based sexual abuse prevention programs. The purpose of the present study was to investigate whether or not parents perceived any harmful effects of having their children participate in a school-based child sexual abuse prevention program. The collection of the data was intended to be preliminary and descriptive in nature.

Method

Subjects

Forty-four parents of children in four grade levels (kindergarten, first, fifth and sixth) served as subjects. Their children attended a public school serving a largely lower-to-middle-class population in a small rural town in eastern Washington.

Measures

This study utilized a Parent's Perceptions Questionnaire developed by the authors. The Parent's Perceptions Questionnaire (PPQ) takes approximately five minutes to complete. It was designed to assess parent's perceptions of the harmful effects of having their children participate in a school-based sexual abuse prevention program. Following is the format of the PPQ.

1. After participating in the program, did your child make any comments to you about the program or ask you any questions about the topic? _____ yes _____ no

2. If yes, please tell us some of the questions asked or comments made: _____

3. In your opinion, did the program have any effect on your child?

_____ yes, it had a good effect

_____ yes, it had a bad effect

_____ no, it had no effect

4. We want to know if your child's behavior has changed in

any way since she/he participated in the program. Since being in the program, has your child:

	Yes	No
a. Had any changes in eating habits?	____	____
b. Had any sleeping problems?	____	____
c. Had any nightmares?	____	____
d. Cried out in his/her sleep?	____	____
e. Been fearful of men?	____	____
f. Been fearful of strangers?	____	____
g. Been fearful of leaving the house?	____	____
h. Been fearful of going to school?	____	____
i. Have there been any changes in the way your child reacts to your physical affection?	____	____
j. Any other changes? (Please describe)	____	____

5. In your opinion, do you think your child understands the concept of child sexual abuse?

_____ yes
_____ no
_____ I don't know

6. Before participating in the program, had you ever discussed the topic of child sexual abuse with your child?

_____ yes
_____ no

Procedure

Children from grades K, 1, 5, and 6, depending on their random group assignment, either watched a film aimed at teaching sexual abuse prevention skills or participated in a behavioral skills training program in which the skills were actively rehearsed (for further details of the programs and assessment devices, see Wurtele, Saslawsky, Miller, Marrs, and Britcher, in press).

One week after participating in the program, the children were asked to deliver a questionnaire to their parents (school policy prohibited direct contact with the parents, thus limiting our ability to insure a large response rate). A letter was attached to each questionnaire requesting that each parent fill out the questionnaire to the best of his/her ability and return it as soon as possible. The parents completed the forms anonymously to increase the rate of return, although they did identify their child's sex, grade, and their relationship to the child. A total of 44 questionnaires (48 percent of total) were returned to the school via U.S. mail with a self-addressed, stamped envelope.

Results

Parents' responses were nominally coded and Fisher exact probability tests were used to compare parents' answers to the questions across the different levels of sex of the child (male vs. female) and age (young = kindergarten and first graders combined vs. old = fifth and six graders combined). No significant differences were found for sex. Only one significant age difference was obtained, that being on Question 4. The parents of younger children were more likely than the parents of older children to mark at least one way in which the program affected their child's behavior (p = .01). Specifically, only one older child's parent reported a behavioral change, whereas five out of the 16 young children's parents reported a change in behavior. Of these five parents, each reported that only one change had occurred. For one of these five parents, the change was that "my daughter became more affectionate, wanting to be held more and kissed more." Of the remaining four parents, two indicated sleeping problems (i.e., "child wanted to sleep with mom and dad because she was cold"; "he cried out in his sleep"), one indicated that the child had been fearful of strangers, and one reported a change in eating habits.

When asked whether their children made any comments to them about the program or asked any questions about the topic, 64 percent of the parents responded affirmatively. The majority of these parents reported that their children simply made comments to them about what they had learned. Several of the older children commented to their parents that they had "already learned about that [sexual abuse]." A few of the younger children expressed embarrassment about participating in the program.

In response to Question 3, "In your opinion, did the program have any effect on your child?" 55 percent of the parents responded that the program had a positive effect, 45 percent stated that the program had no effect, and none reported that the program had a negative effect.

Eighty-eight percent of the parents responded positively to Question 5, "In your opinion, do you think your child understands the concept of child sexual abuse?" Of the remaining parents, 7 percent replied "no," while 5 percent were not sure whether or not their child had an understanding.

The majority of parents surveyed responded affirmatively to Question 6, "Before participating in the program, had you ever discussed the topic of child sexual abuse with your child?" Seventy-nine percent of the parents reported that they had discussed this topic, while the remaining 21 percent of respondents said that they had not discussed the topic with their child prior to program administration.

Discussion

Results of this study demonstrate that parents of children who participated in a school-based child sexual abuse prevention program observed relatively few negative changes in their children's behavior as a result of the program. The questions included in the PPQ concerned behavioral indicants of anxiety and/or depression in the child, along with changes in the way the child related to other people in his/her environment.

These were the feared consequences most frequently expressed to us by parents, yet present results indicate that these fears may be unwarranted. Indeed, 89 percent of the parents did not report any negative changes in their child's behavior as a function of being in the program. Of the five parents of young children who did report a change, only three of the responses could be considered "negative" effects. Thus, only 7 percent of the total sample of parents reported any possible negative side effects of participating in the educational program, and no parent reported that the program had an overall negative effect on his/her child.

Several limitations of our study must be noted. The fact that only half of the parents returned their questionnaires (even though we assured them their anonymity), suggests some possible limitation in generalization of results. However, it would seem that parents who observed any negative effects would be the ones more likely to return the questionnaires. Also, our findings may not be applicable to all sexual abuse educational programs. Children in our program watched a film on the topic and participated in a behavioral skills training package in which modeling, social reinforcement, and practice were employed to teach personal safety skills (Wurtele et al., in press). Thus, the children received a good deal of individualized attention and ample opportunity to discuss the topic and voice their fears and concerns. Ineffective programs which do not adequately teach the children what they can do to protect themselves could foreseeably upset the children and result in many of the behavioral changes included in our questionnaire. In addition, the behavioral changes measured by the PPQ may not be inclusive of all potential negative effects. Other assessment approaches (e.g., individual interviews with the parent and child, observations in the home) may be more sensitive to such effects.

A positive finding from our study was that 64 percent of the parents indicated that their children commented to them about the program. It was hoped that participating in the program would serve as a vehicle for further discussion at home so that the children could obtain additional information and so that the secrecy surrounding the topic could be further diffused. Need for this transfer to the home is evidenced by the fact that almost one-fourth of the parents had not discussed the topic with their children prior to their participating in the program. As with sex education in general, it does not appear that parents are often able or willing to discuss sexual abuse with their children, again supporting the role of the school system in conducting such programs. It is clear that preventing the sexual abuse of our children should be a priority (Finkelhor, 1984), and present results suggest that such programs can be implemented in the schools without harming the children or disrupting their family system.

References

Bartlett, R. (1978). "An Investigation of Child Abuse/Neglect Instruction Offered in Early Childhood and Elementary Education Preservice Programs." (*Dissertation Abstracts International, 38,* (10-A) 6064-6065 (University Microfilms No. 7804506).

Brown, L. (Ed.). (1981). *Sex Education in the Eighties: The Challenge of Healthy Sexual Evolution,* New York: Plenum Press.

Cook, J. (1972). "The Evolution of Sex Education in the Public Schools of the United States, 1900–1970." Unpublished doctoral dissertation, Southern Illinois University (University Microfilms No. 72-24, 353).

Dearth, P. (1974). "Viable Sex Education in the Schools: Expectations of Students, Parents, and Experts." *Journal of School Health, 44,* 190–193.

Department of Health and Human Services. (1981). *National Study of the Incidence and Severity of Child Abuse and Neglect,* Washington, D.C.: U.S. Government Printing Office.

Education Commission of the States. (1978). *Teacher Education: An Active Participant in Solving the Problem of Child Abuse and Neglect,* Denver: Author.

Finkelhor, D. (1979). *Sexually Victimized Children.* New York: Free Press.

Finkelhor, D. (1984). "The Prevention of Child Sexual Abuse: An Overview of Needs and Problems." *SIECUS Report, 13,* 1–5.

Gallup Poll. (1980). *America's Families—1980,* Princeton, N.J.: Gallup Organization.

Gelinas, D. J. (1983). "The Persisting Negative Effects of Incest." *Psychiatry*, *46*, 312–32.

Hale, C., and Gustavus, S. (1978). "The Subtle Points of Controversy: A Case Study in Implementing Sex Education. *Journal of School Health*, *48*, 586–91.

Hazzard, A. (1984). "Training Teachers to Identify and Intervene with Abused Children." *Journal of Clinical Child Psychology*, *13(3)*, 288–93.

Kirby, D., Alter, J., and Scales, P. (1979). *An Analysis of U.S. Sex Education Programs and Evaluation of Methods*. Springfield, Va.: National Technical Information Service.

Lynch, A. (1975). "Child Abuse in the School-Age Population." *Journal of School Health, 45,* 141–48.

McCaffrey, M., and Tewey, S. (1978). "Preparing Educators to Participate in the Community Response to Child Abuse and Neglect." *Exceptional Children, 45,* 114–22.

Mrazek, P. B., and Mrazek, D. A. (1981). "The Effects of Child Sexual Abuse: Methodological Considerations." In P. B. Mrazek and C. H. Kempe (Eds.), *Sexually Abused Children and Their Families* (pp. 235–45). New York: Pergamon Press.

Munson, H. E. (1976). "What Teachers Think They Need to Be Sexuality Educators." *Health Education*, *7*, 31–40.

Pelcovitz, D. (1978). "Child Abuse as Viewed by Suburban Elementary Teachers." *Dissertation Abstracts International*, *38*, (8-A), 4694 (University Microfilms No. 7730239).

Ryan, I. J., and Dunn, P. (1979). "Sex Education from Prospective Teachers' View Poses a Dilemma." *Journal of School Health*, *49*, 573–75.

Scales, P. and Kirby, D. (1983). "Perceived Barriers to Sex Education: A Survey of Professionals." *Journal of Sex Research*, *19(4)*, 309–326.

Wurtele, S. K.; Saslawsky, D.A.; Miller, C. L.; Marrs, S. R.; and Britcher, J. C. (in press). "Teaching Personal Safety Skills for Potential Prevention of Sexual Abuse: A Comparison of Treatments." *Journal of Consulting and Clinical Psychology*.

How Programs Are Evaluated*

Ellen Gray
Joan Di Leonardi

Once there is agreement that primary prevention efforts should be evaluated, the question is: How can this be done? The following outline spells out the essential steps in conducting a program evaluation and will serve as a basis for the discussions that follow.

Steps in Conducting an Evaluation

1. Establish the purpose and audience of the evaluation.
   a. Decide whether the purpose is to refine the process or to measure success; consider what decisions are to be made on the basis of the evaluation.
   b. Determine whether the audience is primarily lay community, professional program staff, outside professionals, or funding sources.
2. Refine program objectives.
   a. Rework objectives until they are clear and specific.
   b. Focus on what can be measured (measurable objectives are usually matters of knowledge, attitudes, or behavior).

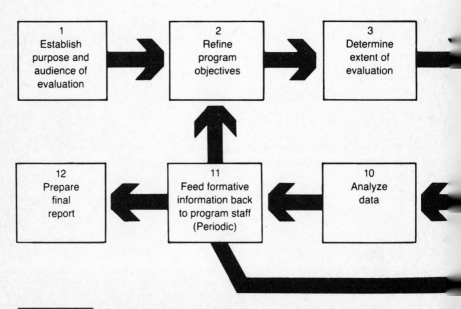

*Reprinted with permission from *Evaluating Child Abuse Prevention Programs* by Ellen Gray and Joan Di Leonardi, © 1982, by permission of the publisher, the National Committee for Prevention of Child Abuse, Chicago, Illinois.

3. Determine the extent of the evaluation.
   a. Assess the cost and difficulty of gathering data.
   b. Assess the cost and difficulty of analyzing data.
   c. Consider the audience for the final report.
4. Develop an evaluation design.
   a. Plan what general data (demographics, output) will be collected and when.
   b. Specify who will be given what test, when, and by whom.
   c. Decide whether service groups will be compared with themselves or with another population as a control group.
5. Find or develop instruments.
   a. Pretest self-developed instruments to get some measure of validity and reliability.
   b. Collect baseline data.
6. Plan an analysis of information.
   a. Make use of the analysis built into established instruments.
   b. For self-developed instruments determine what you want to know about the information collected.
7. Choose a sampling method.
   a. Decide whether all members of a service population or a representative sample will receive the test.

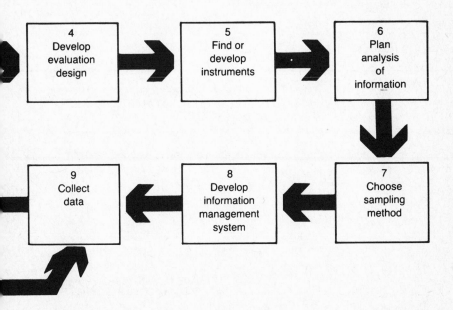

    b. Specify how many will be in the sample.

    c. Establish how members of the sample are to be chosen.

8. Develop an information management system.

    a. Plan how data will get to the evaluator.

    b. Prescribe how often data are to be transmitted.

    c. Stipulate how data will be recorded by the evaluator.

9. Collect data.

    a. Consider points of possible bias.

    b. Take steps to increase interrater reliability.

    c. Collect in such a way as to facilitate later analysis.

10. Analyze data.

    a. Look for changes over time.

    b. Look for differences between groups.

    c. Look for effects of the program.

11. Feed formative information back to program staff. (Periodic)

    a. Prepare component-specific reports.

    b. Interpret the reports for program directors.

    c. If the program does not change as result of this formative evaluation (which may necessitate a change in evaluation design), resume collecting data; if the program does change, go back to step 2.

12. Prepare a final report.

    a. Describe the target population.

    b. Describe the program.

    c. Describe the results.

    d. Interpret the results.

Evaluation Components

Certain terms commonly used by evaluators can be helpful in discussing the components of a primary prevention program evaluation. The terms to be used here include:

Input. Investments in staff and volunteer time, money, training, and other program resources. *Input* is used here to mean any resources used or expended in delivering the primary prevention service.

Output. Units of effort produced by using the resources. Output units can be measured fairly easily. They can include such things as hours of group contact, numbers of lessons completed, costs per service unit, costs of transportation, numbers of media impressions, numbers of requests for information answered or referrals made. They provide a good gauge of the activity of the prevention program and can be used to determine how costly one program is to deliver compared with another. Most service statistics and reports are statements of output. They do not, however, demonstrate whether the service had any effect on the problem to which it was applied.

Outcome. Effects of the interventions on the lives of the people directly involved with the program. To support a statement that someone is doing better in some way because of a program, it is necessary to have a standard of comparison. The comparison group may be the participants themselves before they were part of the program, other people who did not receive the program, or the whole population of similar people. The problems of measuring each of these are discussed in the sections dealing with specific evaluation designs and kinds of programs.

Impact. Changes attributable to the prevention program that go beyond the people directly involved and affect the lives of other people or a whole community. For example, if a successful perinatal program in one hospital leads to adoption of certain birthing and family support practices in all the hospitals of that community, the adoption of those practices is part of the program's impact.

There are difficulties in measuring each of these components. The more information your program can gather and the more of that information you present in the form of outcome or impact evaluation, the more convincing the evidence of program effectiveness will be.

Components of a Program Evaluation

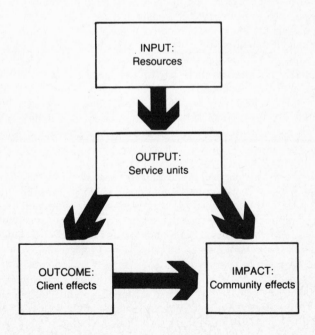

Types of Evaluation

Evaluations commonly are classified into two general types:

Formative evaluation. Done on a continuing or developing program. As information is collected during the course of the evaluation, it is given back to the program staff so that they may adjust the program in the ways indicated. If a new project is community funded and is testing out some primary prevention strategy, a formative evaluation provides ongoing information for program development and thus increases the usefulness of the program. This type of evaluation can and should be a continuous process.

Summative evaluation. Delivered at the end of a stated program period (although it should be planned at the beginning of the program and conducted throughout the program's duration). It is not intended to modify the program but rather to decide how successful or cost effective it is and ultimately whether or not it should be continued. Many projects that receive outside funding, especially from the government, are asked to provide or cooperate with a summative evaluation.

Setting Measurable Objectives

A frequently overlooked or misunderstood step between conceptualization of an idea and successful implementation of a program is setting down the goals and objectives in specific, measurable form. There are some very good reasons for taking the time to complete this step carefully:

- It brings visionary statements of purpose down to a level where tasks become clearer. For what may well be the first time, you can actually get some sense of where to start—and what to do second, third, and fourth.
- If you are being evaluated by an outside evaluator, he or she has only your stated objectives to work from. If they do not reflect what you are really doing, you are not likely to measure up to them. If the evaluators are comparing programs with what they assume are identical goals, and yours are fuzzy or misstated, it will result in the proverbial comparison of apples and oranges.
- If you are conducting your own evaluation, you will not be able to devise useful evaluation instruments if your goals and objectives are not clear and specific. For instance, you cannot measure "organizing the community around the prevention of child abuse" with a questionnaire, nor can you directly survey program participants to determine whether they have "become more aware of themselves as parents."

Objectives can be statements of acquisition or change in knowledge, attitudes, or behavior. *Which* knowledge, *which* attitude, or *which* behavior is to be acquired should be spelled out. A change from what attitude to what attitude, from what behavior to what behavior, should be itemized. And,

158

although long-range goals are useful and nice, it is only those goals and objectives that are achievable and measurable during the evaluation period that can be used for evaluation purposes.

A typically stated objective for a parent education group might be:

To reduce unrealistic expectations of their children on the part of parents participating in the program.

As stated, this is unmeasurable. The question must then be asked: How will this be done? The answer might be:

Parents will be given the rudiments of child development theory.

In terms of knowledge acquisition, then, the objectives can be further broken down to:

On a written test parents will be able to pinpoint the age range in which certain behaviors of children can reasonably be expected to occur.

This objective can be made more specific by giving a sample question:

What is the earliest age at which a child can reasonably be expected to be toilet trained?
  1–6 months
  7–12 months
  13–18 months
  19–24 months
  25–30 months

It is true that acquisition of such knowledge does not necessarily produce any change in attitude or behavior. Change on these two planes must be measured separately. The process of successive narrowing of the objectives, however, would be the same.

Appendices

Appendix A

Physical and Behavioral Indicators

Type of Child Abuse/Neglect	Physical Indicators	Behavioral Indicators
PHYSICAL ABUSE	Unexplained bruises and welts: —on face, lips, mouth —on torso, back, buttocks, thighs —in various stages of healing —clustered, forming regular patterns —reflecting shape of article used to inflict (electric cord, belt buckle) —on several different surface areas —regularly appear after absence, weekend, or vacation —human bite marks —bald spots Unexplained burns: —cigar, cigarette burns, especially on soles, palms, back, or buttocks —immersion burns (sock-like, glove-like, doughnut-shaped on buttocks or genitalia) —patterned like electric burner, iron, etc. —rope burns on arms, legs, neck, or torso Unexplained fractures: —to skull, nose, facial structure —in various stages of healing —multiple or spiral fractures Unexplained lacerations or abrasions: —to mouth, lips, gums, eyes —to external genitalia	Wary of adult contacts Apprehensive when other children cry Behavioral extremes: —aggressiveness, or —withdrawal —overly compliant Afraid to go home Reports injury by parents Exhibits anxiety about normal activities, e.g., napping Complains of soreness and moves awkwardly Destructive to self and others Early to school or stays late as if afraid to go home Accident prone Wears clothing that covers body when not appropriate Chronic runaway (especially adolescents) Cannot tolerate physical contact: or touch
PHYSICAL NEGLECT	Consistent hunger, poor hygiene, inappropriate dress Consistent lack of supervision, especially in dangerous activities or long periods Unattended physical problems or medical needs Abandonment Lice Distended stomach, emaciated	Begging, stealing food Constant fatigue, listlessness or falling asleep States there is no caretaker at home Frequent school absence or tardiness Destructive, pugnacious School dropout (adolescents) Early emancipation from family (adolescents)

# of Child Abuse and Neglect*

Type of Child Abuse/Neglect	Physical Indicators	Behavioral Indicators
SEXUAL ABUSE	Difficulty in walking or sitting Torn, stained or bloody underclothing Pain or itching in genital area Bruises or bleeding in external genitalia, vaginal or anal areas Venereal disease Frequent urinary or yeast infections Frequent unexplained sore throats	Unwilling to participate in certain physical activities Sudden drop in school performance Withdrawal, fantasy or unusually infantile behavior Crying with no provocation Bizarre, sophisticated, or unusual Anorexia (especially adolescents) sexual behavior or knowledge Sexually provocative Poor peer relationships Reports sexual assault by caretaker Fear of or seductiveness toward males Suicide attempts (especially adolescents) Chronic runaway Early pregnancies
EMOTIONAL MALTREAT-MENT	Speech disorders Lags in physical development Failure to thrive (especially in infants) Asthma, severe allergies, or ulcers Substance abuse	Habit disorders (sucking, biting, rocking, etc.) Conduct disorders (antisocial, destructive, etc.) Neurotic traits (sleep disorders, inhibition of play) Behavioral extremes: —compliant, passive —aggressive, demanding Overly adaptive behavior: —inappropriately adult —inappropriately infantile Developmental lags (mental, emotional) Delinquent behavior (especially adolescents)

*Adapted from Broadhurst, D. D.; Edmunds, M.; MacDicken, R. A. *Early Childhood Programs and the Prevention and Treatment of Child Abuse and Neglect.* The User Manual Series. Washington, D.C.: U.S. Department of Health, Education and Welfare, 1979.

Appendix B

Child Sexual Abuse

Abuse and Neglect Statistics

TABLE 1

Reports of Child Abuse and Neglect

	1983	1984	% Increase/ Decrease
Arkansas	10,221	12,558	23%
California	126,855	138,061	9%
Colorado	9,268	8,640	-7%
Delaware	2,550	3,944	55%
Florida	46,851	57,704	23%
Hawaii	3,627	4,361	20%
Idaho	5,939	7,324	23%
Illinois	36,018	39,230	9%
Iowa	14,511	15,838	9%
Kentucky *	33,703*	32,929*	-2%
Louisiana	18,607	20,943	13%
Maine	8,465	10,541	25%
Maryland	6,509	8,301	28%
Massachusetts	36,258	46,393	28%
Michigan	37,561	41,206	10%
Minnesota	11,422	16,667	46%
Mississippi	4,004	4,901	22%
Missouri	34,210	39,709	16%
Nebraska	4,417	6,249	41%
Nevada	5,056	6,146	22%
New Hampshire	2,973	3,955	33%
New Jersey	26,398	44,368	68%
New Mexico	12,600	14,000	11%
New York	74,120	80,990	9%
North Carolina	16,979	17,970	6%
North Dakota	2,364	2,857	21%
Oklahoma	14,997	18,149	21%
Oregon	13,639	16,538	21%
Pennsylvania	15,872	20,088	27%
Rhode Island	3,365	5,470	63%
South Carolina	12,931	14,171	10%
South Dakota	5,577	6,536	17%
Texas	58,965	64,313	9%
Utah	8,423	8,945	6%
Vermont	1,865	2,144	15%
Virginia	40,581	42,842	6%
Washington	36,652	42,352	16%
West Virginia	12,396	11,183	-10%
Wisconsin	9,614	17,728	84%
Wyoming	2,054	2,346	14%
Total	828,417	958,590	16%

* Figure denotes number of children. This state treats each victim of child abuse/neglect as a separate case.

Tables 1, 2, and 3 from *Too Young to Run: The Status of Child Abuse in America*. New York: Child Welfare League of America, 1986. Reprinted with permission.

TABLE 2
Reports of Child Sexual Abuse

	1983	1984	Percent Increase
Arkansas	1,327	2,231	68%
Delaware	184	358	95%
Hawaii	303	540	78%
Idaho	498	970	95%
Illinois	3,178	4,352	37%
Iowa	1,568	2,127	36%
Kentucky *	1,676*	2,390*	43%
Louisiana	1,853	3,204	73%
Maryland	1,300	2,290	76%
Minnesota	2,462	4,357	77%
Missouri	2,573	4,050	57%
New Mexico	330	439	33%
New York	4,331	6,859	58%
North Dakota	190	307	62%
Oregon	1,549	3,551	129%
South Carolina	1,236	1,538	24%
Utah	611	941	54%
Washington	7,300	9,491	30%
Wisconsin	2,197	5,106	132%
Wyoming	348	495	42%
Total	35,014	55,596	59%

* Figure denotes number of children. This state treats each victim of child abuse/neglect as a separate case.

TABLE 3
Reports of Sexual Abuse as a Percentage of Abuse and Neglect Reports

State	1983 Abuse & Neglect Reports	1983 Sexual Abuse Reports	%	1984 Abuse & Neglect Reports	1984 Sexual Abuse Reports	%
Arkansas	10,221	1,327	13%	12,558	2,231	18%
Delaware	2,550	184	7%	3,944	358	9%
Hawaii	3,627	303	8%	4,361	540	12%
Idaho	5,939	498	8%	7,324	970	13%
Illinois	36,018	3,178	9%	39,230	4,352	11%
Iowa	14,511	1,568	11%	15,838	2,127	13%
Kentucky *	33,705*	1,676*	5%	32,929*	2,390*	7%
Louisiana	18,607	1,853	10%	20,943	3,204	15%
Maryland	6,509	1,300	20%	8,301	2,290	28%
Minnesota	11,422	2,462	22%	16,667	4,357	26%
Missouri	34,210	2,573	8%	39,709	4,050	10%
New Mexico	12,600	330	3%	14,000	439	3%
New York	74,120	4,331	6%	80,990	6,859	8%
North Dakota	2,364	190	8%	2,857	307	11%
Oregon	13,639	1,549	11%	16,538	3,551	21%
South Carolina	12,931	1,236	10%	14,171	1,538	11%
Utah	8,423	611	7%	8,945	941	11%
Washington	36,652	7,300	20%	42,352	9,491	22%
Wisconsin	9,614	2,197	23%	17,728	5,106	29%
Wyoming	2,054	348	17%	2,346	495	21%
Total	349,714	35,014	10%	401,731	55,596	14%

* Figure denotes number of children. This state treats each victim of child abuse/neglect as a separate case.

Interagency Task Force on Child Abuse, Worcester Public Schools: A Preventive Implementation*

by Claire L. Angers

As a former guidance counselor and now an elementary school principal in an urban school system. I have come to recognize the importance of involvement by school personnel in the issue of child abuse. The following recounts a series of events that led to this personal realization.

During the 1982–1983 school year there were several severe cases of child abuse in which the principal and I (as the elementary counselor of Grafton Street School) were intensely involved. Despite many concerted efforts at intervention and indications of possible serious consequences to come, we were unable to successfully intervene in an abuse case that eventually concluded in a youngster's death.

This event served as a catalyst for affirming our need to address some very serious situations by notifying higher school department officials of their existence. Thus we wrote a position paper on child abuse and sent it to Dr. John Durkin, Superintendent of Schools.

Later during that same school year, an article appeared in the *Worcester Telegram* indicating that Governor Dukakis was convening a "major interagency policy group" dealing with the issue of child abuse. Because it appeared clear to us that school systems were not going to be represented in this group, we forwarded a letter dated May 13, 1983, to the elementary supervisor relative to our concerns.

As a result, the superintendent of schools contacted the governor, and both the principal (Daniel O'Neil) and I (a guidance counselor at that time) were appointed to the Governor's Task Force on Child Abuse, on which we would serve from 1983 until 1985.

In the summer of 1983, a similar task force was implemented in Worcester at the request of the superintendent. This group consisted of a member of the school committee, various school administrators, representatives from the Department of Social Services, the police department, and a community agency adept at presenting sexual abuse prevention programs. Our task was to discuss implementation of a prevention program centered around the issue of sexual abuse as it pertains to an overall safety program within the public school system.

This group met for an entire year and had many discussions about the appropriateness of the subject matter for school presentation. By October of 1984, three principals were serving on the committee, including the writer, as the newly appointed principal of

---

*Reprinted with permission of the author.

Grafton Street School. Several committee members viewed a presentation to a group of youngsters of a role play dealing with the overall issue of safety and the particular area of sexual abuse prevention. Impressed with the sensitive manner in which the delicate subject matter was presented, the committee felt safe in proceeding. I volunteered to have my school become the pilot school. Thus the following four-part program was implemented:

1. The Department of Social Services and the police department gave an in-service presentation to the entire faculty about the issue of child abuse, and sexual abuse in particular.

2. The community agency presenters gave an in-service program to our entire school staff specifically about the program that would be delivered to our children. They also addressed any issues raised by faculty members.

3. The community agency presented the material to the parents and answered questions. At this time parents were given the option of having their children included in the program. Although many had questions, no parent refused participation on behalf of his/her child.

4. The community agency's program was presented to individual classrooms with various faculty members present.

Before any further implementation, the committee met to discuss the presentation and its effectiveness and appropriateness. The school department's newly developed "School-Based Procedures for Reporting Suspected Cases of Child Abuse" was distributed to all schools to inform all personnel of the proper means of addressing this sensitive issue. The most important aspects of these reporting procedures are as follows:

1. A child reports an incident of abuse to a teacher.

2. The teacher's task is to try to convince the child to come with him/her to the principal to report the incident to the principal directly.

3. The principal then assumes all responsibility, thereby allowing the teacher to preserve the invaluable interpersonal relationship with the child. It is important that this be preserved in order to safeguard the pupil-teacher rapport so essential to daily interaction in the classroom.

4. The principal informs the child of all the steps and procedures involved, as well as possible outcomes and the reasons therefor. Sensitivity to the affective needs of the child is essential.

5. The principal reports the incident of alleged abuse by phone to the Department of Social Services and follows up with a written report within 24 hours.

6. The principal informs the parent, in person (if at all possible), of the report, the reasons why, and possible outcomes, with the overall emphasis on acquiring help for the child and his/her family.

By the spring of 1986, nine elementary schools in Worcester had received the entire four-part program and another three schools had received the first component (Department of Social Services and police department).

At this time, the community agency informed us that it was separating from its main funding source and it would need additional funding. Until this point, Grafton Street School was funded by the agency because it wanted to become involved in the schools. (Two of the schools were funded through a $4,000 grant written through the Chapter 1 office of the Worcester Public Schools; the remaining six of the nine schools were funded through grants secured through the community agency.)

When the agency presented its projected budget to us, it was much more than the school department could allocate. The office of program development allocated $6,000, to be used in the 1986–1987 school year for a prevention program.

As we began to examine our own delivery of services, questions began to arise with respect to the following issues:

1. What happens after the initial prevention presentation relative to followup?

2. The community group presenters are looked upon as confidants; however, there is little or no transference of roles to classroom teachers in order to provide ongoing support.

As a result of this process of introspection, we began to look at a model for training classroom teachers to do the presentations and training backup personnel (such as counselors and nurses) as presenters in the event that a teacher felt unable or unwilling to handle the delicate material appropriately.

The committee then sent a notice asking for "Proposals for a Prevention Program in Worcester Public Schools" to all the local agencies. After receiving four proposals, we invited representatives of these four agencies to present their proposals to our committee. The committee forwarded to the superintendent of schools the recommendation of the Escape/Access program, which uses the Personal Safety Curriculum. (See Appendix I of this publication.)

On August 14, 1986, the school committee, in a unanimous vote, approved the implementation of the Escape/Access Program in all 40 elementary schools during the 1986–1987 school year.

Currently we are in the implementation stages, but are pleased with the progress to date. Our interagency committee continues to meet and evaluate our efforts.

The implementation has followed a set process:

1. The program was explained to interested principals at an interagency committee meeting to which they were invited.

2. Teachers received a two-and-a-half hour training given by Escape/Access during the teachers' released time day.

3. The Department of Social Services and the police department gave presentations on their involvement in the helping process to teachers.

4. Nurses and pupil personnel received the above training.

5. An open meeting was held to acquaint parents with the program.

6. The program is being implemented with the children.

7. A review of the program results with the principals and the interagency committee will be made.

I have recounted how one city undertook the implementation of a preventive program. I recognize that each geographic area is different; however, I hope others will find this explanation of our efforts useful in formulating their own plans.

As one who was intimately involved in this process, I will say that the implementation of such a plan, and all it entails, seems overwhelming at times. Ours is a large urban school system with 40 elementary schools. The planning and implementation process is extremely time consuming. It is often difficult to ensure that this process does not detract from other important areas in one's work, and that it is kept in the proper perspective.

One cannot deny that the nature of the subject of abuse in itself is distasteful and, although important, is not something that one readily chooses to become involved with. There are times when it is necessary to disassociate oneself from the entire issue for some therapeutic relief. One must never lose sight of the end product, however: if children can be educated in this area, they can be protected without being unduly alarmed.

Finally, the political and social climate of the community must be recognized and addressed. One must strive to meet the challenge of sometimes confronting and sometimes working within the bureaucratic structure while also addressing and advocating for the special needs of some very needy children. The key and ultimate challenge lies in positive, cooperative, and sensitive "manipulation" of the bureaucratic structure in such a way that it recognizes and adequately addresses the needs of children in today's society.

The process has been invigorating for all the committee members. The challenge is worthwhile. It is our hope that other schools will be encouraged by our successes and will learn from our setbacks, and that together we can influence the future of our children.

Caring for Abused Preschoolers*

Anna C. Salter
Curtis M. Richardson
Steven W. Kairys

Young children who have been physically or emotionally abused seem particularly vulnerable and evoke in us a hope to rescue them from their misfortune. Abused children, however, have learned to distrust their caretakers and have acquired a formidable array of defenses to protect their fragile sense of self. Fantasies of salvation often collide with the realities of caring for a stubborn, negative child who rigidly resists intervention and alienates those who would help.

The damaging impact of maltreatment on children's cognition and affect is explored here, and guidelines for providing care and alleviating the specific skill deficits of abused preschoolers are discussed. Although a number of the illustrations of techniques recommended by the authors have been drawn from work in group preschool settings, the guidelines are intended for use by caregivers who work with these youngsters individually (e.g., in foster homes) or in groups (e.g., in day care centers).

Impact of Abuse

Abused children behave in ways that are typical of any child who is under chronic stress; what is unique is the frequency, severity, and intractability of their behavior patterns.

Unfortunately, much of the research on the physical and emotional effects of child abuse is derived from poorly controlled, retrospective studies. Further, these studies have generally involved small samples and have had little or no longitudinal tracking of the young victims' characteristics [Toro 1982]. The latter is important in that a small-scale 8-year study of matched abused and nonabused samples done by Elmer [1977] indicated that socioeconomic status (SES) and other social stresses were more important than maltreatment in determining a youngster's developmental course. As Toro [1982] has noted, researchers need to define more precisely the extent, type, and frequency of the abuse that has occurred; to include more upper SES children in their samples; to try to distinguish whether developmental deficits preceded abuse or appeared as sequelae; and to apply the most valid and reliable research tools to larger numbers of subjects. The reader is cautioned that some of the information that follows is almost anecdotal in nature and awaits confirmation in prospective, carefully controlled investigations.

---

*Reprinted by special permisison of the Child Welfare League of America from *Child Welfare*, vol. 64, no. 4, July–August 1985. pp. 343–56.

Effects of Physical and Emotional Abuse

Physical and emotional abuse may leave irreversible, somatic stigmata. Martin [1976], in a 5-year, uncontrolled study of 58 physically abused children, found that half (53%) had some neurological damage, of which one-third (31%) had sequelae severe enough to handicap everyday functions. The handicaps included visual and auditory defects, motor impairment, and problems with coordination. Other studies have also substantiated these somatic effects of abuse [Caffey 1972; Baron et al. 1970; Elmer and Gregg 1967].

In and of itself, emotional neglect has been shown to alter the body's production of growth hormone, resulting in a very small child who will always be small. This syndrome has been labeled psychosocial dwarfism [Kotelchuck 1980].

Effect on Development

Evidence as to the impact of maltreatment on motor development in children is mixed. Relich and associates [1980] observed 13 matched pairs of physically abused preschoolers and controls while they played and talked with their mothers. Few differences were found between the groups' movement and social contact behaviors. In contrast, Appelbaum [1977] compared 30 physically abused children to 30 matched controls and found that the former had significantly poorer gross motor development as measured by the Bayley Scales of Infant Development and the Denver Developmental Screening Test. The gross motor delays were obvious in subjects as young as 4 months of age. Martin [1976] also observed gross motor deficits in his sample and theorized that these were a consequence of a home environment that discouraged youngsters from exploring or taking risks (e.g., running, balancing, hopping, skipping, and riding a tricycle).

In addition, delays in speech and language have been identified. Martin [1976:80] noted that younger abused children have more noticeable communication deficits. Children from ages 2 or 3 to 5, he asserted, "get into trouble for talking." Thus they refrain from practicing speech. In fact, much of their communication is nonverbal. Further, they perform concrete, verbal tasks far better than more abstract, unstructured ones. Martin warns those who test abused children's language skills not to be misled by adaptive responses to the testing situation; these may suggest better language skills than the children actually have. Allen and Oliver [1982] investigated the language skills of three sets of abused preschoolers: those who had been physically abused ($n = 13$); those who had only been neglected ($n = 7$); and those who had been both abused and neglected ($n = 31$). Neglect was found to be a good predictor of the child's auditory comprehension and verbal ability. This suggests that lack of stimulation and support are critical factors affecting language delays.

Effect on Cognition

As early as the late 1960s, a significant I.Q. decrease in children who had been physically abused was documented [Elmer and Gregg 1967]. Martin [1976] evaluated the I.Q. of 58 abused children and found more than twice the expected number of youngsters with an I.Q. of less than 85. Thirty-five percent (35%; $n = 19$) of his sample had I.Q.s below 85, in contrast to 15% of the normal population. Sandgrund and associates [1974:329] compared 60 abused, 30 neglected, and 30 nonabused children ages 5 to 12. A disproportionate number of the abused and neglected children had I.Q.s below 70. These investigators noted that it "remains to be shown conclusively whether cognitive impairment antedates abuse or is one of its effects."

Martin [1976:88–101] also theorized that cognitive delays may be attributable to the unpredictable, unstimulating, nonsupportive, even dangerous environment in which abused children live. Such an environment causes them to become anxious, preoccupied with fantasy, or focused on finding ways to survive. In testing situations, Martin [1976:116–120] has noted how, among other characteristics, fear of failure, difficulty in absorbing instructions, and failure to scan handicap the abused child. Obviously, such traits impede learning in general.

Effect on Affect

Abused children have learned that their world is an unpredictable, often hurtful place. The adults who care for them may be angry, impatient, depressed, and distant. Further, they can be transformed, without warning, into hostile, violent persons. The child is beset with fears of harsh punishment, verbal deprecation, and abandonment, and must be prepared to anticipate and meet the needs of his or her parents [Martin 1976].

This overwhelming assault on the child's ego leads to major affective disturbances as youngsters employ a variety of pathological defenses: avoidance, projection, self-destructive behavior, and hyperaggressiveness [Green 1981]. Maltreated children often look unhappy and appear to take little pleasure in their surroundings [Lynch 1978]. Many exhibit evidence of a masked depression. In a preschooler, this can take the form of sleep disturbances, bed wetting, phobias, apathy, and underachievement [Blumberg 1981].

Frustration, helplessness, fears of abandonment, and scapegoating can all contribute to lowered self-esteem or an innate sense of badness. Abused children tend to adopt the rigid and punitive values of their parents; they become harsh and uncompromising in judging their own actions and those of their playmates [Green 1983; Martin 1976]. Kinard [1982] found that the severity of inflicted injuries was related to children's expression of extrapunitive aggression and poor self-concept. These traits were also more pronounced if the abuse occurred before the child was 3 years old. Thus, internalization of the parental value system interferes with their ability to develop relationships and enjoy life.

Effect on Behavior

Children who have been abused do not behave differently from other youngsters under stress. Several studies [Douglas 1975; Quinton and Rutter 1976; Rutter 1979; Rutter and Quinton 1977] have indicated that the number, not the type, of stresses in a child's life strongly affect the risk for developing some form of psychiatric disorder in later childhood.

Indeed, a review of studies of children's psychiatric symptoms found that children's behavior was generally described in one of two ways: "internalizing" or "overcontrolled" (i.e., inhibited, shy, anxious) behaviors and "externalizing" or "undercontrolled" (i.e., acting out, aggressive) behaviors [Achenbach and Edelbrock 1978]. This was true regardless of the source of the behavior rating (e.g., mental health worker, parent, teacher) and, presumably, irrespective of the etiology of the behavior, since the study samples were mostly drawn from general clinic populations. Although it is not clear why one child under stress will withdraw while another will become aggressive, it seems reasonable to consider the impact of temperament.

Investigators who have specifically focused on the behavior of abused children have found externalizing and internalizing behaviors in children of various ages. Physically and verbally aggressive behavior has been reported in abused children from age 1 through adolescence [Galdston 1971; George and Main 1979; Gaensbauer and Sands 1979; Green 1978a, b]. The targets of aggression have included teachers, peers, and objects, and expression of hostility has sometimes been accompanied by pleasurable affect [Green 1981].

Some studies have also noted depression, avoidance of caretaker-initiated contact, and withdrawal among abused children [Blumberg 1981; George and Main 1979; Martin 1976; Green 1981, 1983; Martin and Beezley 1977]. Galdston [1965] described diminished appetites for food and human contact among abused children. Several reports have noted self-destructive behavior, including suicide attempts. Green [1978c] estimated that 40% of his study sample had hurt themselves in some manner, frequently after separation from parental figures or following beatings by parents. Occasionally, self-destructive behavior occurred during a panic state, a frame of mind that could appear in anticipation of, before, or during an assault.

An exception to the pattern of reports on externalizing and internalizing behavior was reported by Yates [1981], who described three groups of abused children: (1) frightened (the most numerous); (2) angry; and (3) "private." The latter were described as having some ego functions that were precocious and some alarming deficits, particularly in certain relationship skills. They were attractive, bright, eager to please, very cognizant of hospital routine, sensitive to the roles and authority of various staff, and adept at manipulating people and finding sources of nurturance. Although their cognitive skills were good, their peer relationships were poor.

Guidelines for Intervention

Assisting abused preschoolers requires many of the same approaches and techniques as working with other children, only "more so." These youngsters need more consistency, more patience, more time, and more clarity. Children who have not suffered trauma may respond despite inconsistency and ambiguity and usually pick up plenty of information from the environment as to whether adults actively intervene or not. Abused children need more from the caretakers.

All children need help learning limits. Abused children are frequently aggressive, either because they are undersocialized and have simply not learned appropriate social behaviors or because they have acquired negative behaviors. Changing how they behave requires active intervention, but of a sort that does not frighten them or make them feel guilty or bad about themselves.

The remainder of this article is devoted to techniques that the authors recommend to caretakers of abused preschoolers. Readers are reminded that the guidelines can be used in a variety of settings (e.g., foster home, respite care home, group day care home, or preschool center). Regardless of the number of children being cared for, the provider should bear in mind that the level of intervention required to meet abused preschoolers' needs makes individual attention for many activities highly desirable.

Latitude

Stay on the same latitude as the child when giving instructions or setting limits. Bend down next to the youngster and talk directly to her or him in a quiet voice. Preschool children are still in the Piagetian stage called preoperational. They do not override perception with logical operations that tell them, for example, that distance does not alter the strength of a request. An adult speaking to them from a distance of 6 inches seems more compelling than one yelling from across a room. For children of that age, "what you see is what you get." They can be thought of as being perceptually seduced by proximal clues that grab their attention.

Body Language

Be aware of other aspects of your body English, as well as latitude. It is often said that adults cannot fool children, but a more accurate statement might be that adults cannot fool youngsters by words alone. An upset adult can still calm a frightened child if the adult's body language is relaxed. A student teacher, for example, was unable to get a child to come in after outside play time. The child raced around the grounds on a tricycle, ignoring requests to put the toy away. Finally, the head teacher pointed out that the student teacher was saying "Time to come in now" tentatively, as if it were a question. Her reticence and the fact that she stayed outside with the child implied that she expected the youngster to disobey. The head teacher simply walked outside and said the same words in a way that left no doubt that the child would come in. As the head teacher turned and walked back inside, the child put the tricycle away.

On another occasion, the noise level in the preschool room increased when the student teacher was alone with the children. She debated various courses of action, but could think of no positive way to bring the noise level down. Ultimately, the head teacher walked in and quietly went from group to group, making up some reason to chat in a voice barely above a whisper. Each group's noise level dropped as the children struggled to hear the teacher's words. The noise level of the entire room quickly declined, almost as if air had gone out of a balloon.

Positive Phrasing

Word things positively rather than negatively. This may feel awkward initially and takes some practice. Say, for example: "Put your feet on the floor" instead of "Don't stand on the table." "Don't throw sand" translates into "The sand stays in the sandbox." This draws the child's attention to what he or she should be doing rather than what is wrong. Since children tend to fixate on things, positive phrasing has the advantage of distracting them from what they should not be doing (e.g., throwing the cars and trucks) to what they ought to be doing (e.g., keeping the cars and trucks on the floor).

Defining Limits

Set limits on acceptable behavior by identifying what the child wants to accomplish. Once you know what the child needs or wants, you can help him or her to develop options other than sheer aggression. For example, a good response to a fight over toys might be: "Hold it. I think you both want to play with the blocks. Now, we're going to have to figure out another way to solve this problem other than throwing the blocks at each other."

Giving Options

When giving children choices, start simply (e.g., "I'll tell you what. You can have half the blocks and you can have half the blocks."). Over time, move toward giving children a couple of options to choose from (e.g., "OK, how do you want to solve this? Do you want to split the blocks or take turns using the timer?"). Again, over time, allow the children to generate some of their own options (e.g., "OK, you guys, now how are we going to settle this? We could split the blocks by color or number. We could take turns using the timer. Do you have other ideas?"). The day arrives, one hopes, when you can say (not from across the room): "All right, you figure it out, and let me know how you're going to settle it." This gradual approach teaches the child how to solve problems, increasing his or her independence from adult intervention.

Logical Consequences

Work on the principle of logical consequences. Generally, the logical consequence for misusing an activity is removal from that activity. For example, the logical consequence of throwing sand is: "You're telling me you're not ready to play in the sandbox right now. You can try again later." Smearing food in another child's hair necessitates removing the child from the table. Take the position that you are terribly sorry that the child isn't able to continue the activity at the moment. The child will probably get the hang of it later. This avoids power struggles in that the issue is between the child and the consequence, not between the child and you.

Recognize Repeated Problems

When a child is consistently having trouble, remember that there is always a pattern. Note when the child falls apart. Is it when he or she is tired? Is it over meals or before meals? Is it first thing in the morning or last thing in the day? Is it when the child tries to enter groups or when he or she has finished with one thing and is about to start another? Is it when the child is bored or frustrated by something that is too difficult?

Once you know the pattern, you can anticipate when the child will have trouble and begin to help him or her avoid the problem. For instance, a child who is at loose ends at the beginning of the day can be helped by saying "When I don't know what to do in the morning, I just walk around the room and see what kinds of activities we have today. Want to come? Let's see. We have blocks, and, oh yes, there's finger painting and, of course, the cars and trucks." Few children make it all the way around the room without getting absorbed in something. Again, this technique teaches the child skills rather than doing something for the child. As with many problems, it is always more effective to prevent something from happening than to mop up afterward. The teacher who catches the fist in the air is in better shape than the one who catches the fist after it has landed and says: "We don't do that." The child's logical thought is: "What do you mean *we*? I just did."

Identify Feelings

Differentiate between feelings and behavior. You may have to set clear limits on behavior, but always express your acceptance of feelings. For example, it helps to say: "I know you're angry, and that's OK. Everybody gets angry sometimes, but the sand still stays in the sandbox. It's not OK to throw sand in people's eyes." For small children, feelings and behavior are the same thing. If hitting someone with a hammer is wrong, then being angry is wrong. Since they cannot help being angry at times, life becomes very confusing. It is a developmentally important step for children to learn that they can be angry and still control their behavior. (Obviously, many adults have not mastered this developmental task, and some of these adults abuse children.) Abused youngsters, in particular, have had poor models for impulse control. Thus, it becomes especially important to find ways carefully and frequently to emphasize the differences between feelings and actions.

176

Label Feelings

Do not expect that the abused child has verbal labels for his or her feelings and an understanding of what causes them. Label feelings and describe situations in words. Remember also that children, like the rest of us, regress when upset; expect a child's cognitive skills to drop sharply when he or she is distressed. You may have been dealing with a 5-year-old a few minutes ago, but you are dealing with an angry 2-year-old now. Cause-and-effect are more typical of adult logic than child logic. Add the regression caused by strong affect to the cognitive complexity of cause-and-effect and you have a child lost in the impulse of the moment. Such a child is likely to be oblivious to how the whole thing started and have no sense of choices about how to respond. For example, you might say: "I know you're angry. I can tell by the look on your face and by the fact that you're trying to hit him. I bet you're angry because he pulled your hair. I have an idea why he did that. Remember, just a minute ago, you grabbed his art paper and drew marks on it. I've got a funny feeling that what you did made him angry and that's why he hit you."

Promote Assertiveness

Encourage abused children to stand up to each other and back them when they do (e.g., "Tell him you do not want him to draw on your paper."). Initially, the aggressor may only listen because you are literally standing behind the victim, but the notion that people have rights and can assert them appropriately and effectively is important. These are youngsters whose personal rights have been violated; they need to have a place where this does not happen.

Words Versus Action

Some dilemmas are best handled without words. For example, the most effective strategy for a clinging child is to sit down in the middle of the room and make yourself as boring as possible. This is much more effective than trying to leave the child. Threatened with losing you, the child will cling more. Instead, let the child leave you.

Power Struggles

Power struggles are occasionally unavoidable. Sometimes subtle approaches do not work and clear limits have to be set. When possible, however, avoid power struggles. Many potential problems can be reframed in such a way that the conflict never materializes (e.g., "Let's get this stuff put away. We can't have juice until we have a place to put it." Or, "Put your coat on, and I'll race you on the playground.").

If you do get in a power struggle, win it. Children do not feel safe around adults who cannot control them; they feel out of control and anxious. If it takes all day, even if you get nothing else done that day, win the struggle. Further, maintain a matter-of-fact attitude so that the child does not perceive you as gloating over the victory.

Should all else fail, a preschooler can be physically removed from an area or held so that he or she does not assault another child. This is the advantage of dealing with these issues when children are 4 rather than 14. You can be in control physically of a 4-year-old, if you absolutely must.

Positive Endings—and Beginnings

At the end of the day, find something positive that the child did and comment on it. This may be difficult. Still, all children do something positive each day, even if it is only looking at a book for 10 seconds or not hitting someone for that amount of time. When children go home, they then will remember more of what was done right and less of what was done wrong. This will increase the probability that youngsters will see themselves as capable of doing well.

Moreover, start each day new. Do not carry over punishments from day to day. Make it clear to the child that every day is a fresh beginning and that what has happened yesterday is in the past.

Skill Building

Abused children need specific attention paid to skill deficits. Preschool programs that provide a rich array of materials and let the children play are wonderful for those with good learning skills. Abused children, however, often do not have sufficient skill to learn from the environment on their own; they have turned off the environment out of fear or in anger.

Positive regard is an essential ingredient in the skill-building process. Martin [1976:187] notes that treatment of developmental delays requires that the adult show consistent liking for the child regardless of his or her accomplishments; avoid too much emphasis on performance and progress; "hang in there" when the child doesn't "act right"; listen for the youngster's expression of feelings; and do not become upset or overwhelmed if the child wants to talk about the abuse he or she has endured.

Of course, skill building also depends on content. Teachers can help by arranging minilearning episodes presented as games. These episodes may be only a few minutes long, but ought to have a goal, at least in the teacher's mind. The basic preschool curriculum—matching; counting; learning colors, shapes, letters, and numbers—can all, with a little thought, be broken down into learning episodes (e.g., "Let's count the number of forks we'll need for lunch." Or "How many circles can you see in this room?"). In particular, abused preschoolers frequently need help with deficits in two areas: language and gross motor skills.

178

Language

Abused children generally do not speak very much. Encourage them to verbalize by modeling and making comments to them rather than asking questions. Asking questions can be very threatening. Make sure that the child is constantly spoken to, but that little is being demanded. For example, you might say: "Julie is going on the swing. Up and down. She has a yellow dress on today. Now she's sliding down." This sort of monologue may sound strange and stilted to an adult, but doesn't seem to bother children at all. Youngsters invariably begin to talk more when approached in this way.

When you feel it is all right to ask questions of a child with limited language skills, avoid rhetorical, middle-class questions. "How are you today?" is a ritualistic question. One either knows the code or one doesn't; children with limited language skills frequently do not.

Label everything in sight with words. Find excuses to name things, colors, feelings, and concepts.

Correct mispronunciations indirectly instead of telling the child that he or she has made a mistake. Just try to use the word immediately afterward and say it correctly without commenting on the child's efforts (e.g., "Is the yellow yion gone?" "Yes, the yellow *lion* is missing today."). This may not seem face-saving to adults, but it seems to be for children. They hear the word correctly without the ignominy of being corrected.

Use complex words, but then say the same thing in simpler words (e.g., "Yes, she was frustrated. She was upset because she couldn't do the puzzle.").

Gross Motor Skills

Give abused children many opportunities to engage in nonthreatening gross motor play. One way to accomplish this is to organize noncompetitive activities in which performance anxiety is minimal. Chances to swing, slide, jump (e.g., into leaves); climb over and through objects; and ride (e.g., tricycles) are beneficial. Circle games or exercise periods in which children mimic movements are also useful.

When gross motor play has an element of competition, it should be arranged so that youngsters have observable successes. Scavenger hunts, for example, can include looking for objects that are certain to be found. Complex games such as kickball can be broken down into more easily achievable tasks: running from base to base; carrying, bowling, bouncing, throwing, stopping, and catching a ball. Large plastic soda bottles filled with sand can be knocked over by balls that are thrown or bowled from various distances. The rules of thumb are that tasks ought to be easily accomplished and children not be singled out in front of their peers.

Use daily chores to allow children to practice gross motor skills. For example, given a chair of his or her own, the child can move it to different locations in conjunction with changes in classroom or home activities. A young "helper" can carry dishes across the room and arrange them on a shelf or table.

Help children with tasks that they cannot accomplish on their own. Some tasks, such as dressing, may prove frustrating unless the adult and child work as a team. For example, the youngster may be able to pull on shoes arranged by an adult as to right and left and, then, tighten up the laces. Even if the adult ties the laces, the task can be shared; inventing a short story or saying that the child can verbalize as you tie the laces gives him or her a role. The key is to have the child be a participant in and complete as many actions as possible.

Conclusion

Abused children, like other youngsters who have experienced serious childhood stresses, need carefully structured assistance to enable them to maximize learning and engage constructively with caretakers and peers. Otherwise, aggressive and/or withdrawn behavior will impair their efforts to develop good relationships and learn from stimulating environments, even long after the abuse has ended. Without a structured program, the abused child and the caretaker are both likely to experience mutual frustration and a sense of failure. The guidelines for intervention offered here are the keys to effective and rewarding work with young victims of abuse and neglect.

References

Achenbach, Thomas M., and Edelbrock, Craig S. "The Classification of Child Psychopathology: A Review and Analysis of Empirical Efforts." *Psychological Bulletin* 85, 6 (1978): 1275–1301.

Allen, Rebecca E., and Oliver, J. M. "The Effects of Child Maltreatment on Language Development." *Child Abuse and Neglect* 6, 3, (1982): 229–305.

Appelbaum, Alan S. "Developmental Retardation in Infants as a Concomitant of Physical Child Abuse." *Journal of Abnormal Child Psychology* 5 (December 1977): 417–23.

Baron, Michael A.; Bajar, Rafael L.; and Sheaff, Peter J. "Neurologic Manifestations of the Battered Child Syndrome." *Pediatrics* 45 (June 1970): 1003–1007.

Blumberg, Marvin L. "Depression in Abused and Neglected Children." *American Journal of Psychotherapy* 35 (July 1981): 332–335.

Caffey, John. "On the Theory and Practice of Shaking Infants: Its Potential Residual Affects of Permanent Brain Damage and Mental Retardation." *American Journal of Diseases of Childhood* 124 (August 1972): 161–169.

Douglas, J. W. B. "Early Hospital Admissions and Later Disturbances of Behavior and Learning." *Developmental Medicine and Child Neurology* 17 (August 1975): 456–480.

Elmer, Elizabeth. *Fragile Families, Troubled Children: The Aftermath of Infant Trauma*. Pittsburgh, PA: University of Pittsburgh Press, 1977.

Elmer, Elizabeth, and Gregg, Grace S. "Developmental Characteristics of Abused Children." *Pediatrics* 40 (October 1967): 596–602.

Gaensbauer, Theodore, and Sands, Karen. "Distorted Affective Communications in Abused/Neglected Infants and Their Potential Impact on Caretakers." *Journal of the American Academy of Child Psychiatry* 18, 1–4 (1979): 236–250.

180

Galdston, Richard. "Observations on Children Who Have Been Physically Abused and Their Parents." *American Journal of Psychiatry* 122 (October 1965): 440–443.

_____. "Violence Begins at Home." *Journal of the American Academy of Child Psychiatry* 10 (April 1971): 336–350.

George, Carol, and Main, Mary. "Social Interactions of Young Abused Children: Approach, Avoidance, and Aggression." *Child Development* 50 (June 1979): 306–318.

Green, Arthur H. "Child Abuse: Dimension of Psychological Trauma in Abused Children." *Journal of the American Academy of Child Psychiatry* 22 (May 1983): 231–237.

_____. "Core Affective Disturbance in Abused Children." *Journal of the American Academy of Child Psychoanalysis* 9 (July 1981): 435–446.

_____. "Psychopathology of Abused Children." *Journal of the American Academy of Child Psychiatry* 17 (January 1978a): 92–103.

_____. "Psychiatric Treatment of Abused Children." *Journal of Child Psychiatry* 17 (Winter 1978b): 356–371.

_____. "Self-Destructive Behavior in Battered Children." *American Journal of Psychiatry* 135 (May 1978c): 579–582.

Kinard, E. Milling. "Experiencing Child Abuse: Effects on Emotional Adjustment." *American Journal of Orthopsychiatry* 52 (January 1982): 81–90.

Kotelchuck, Milton. "Nonorganic Failure to Thrive: The State of Interactional and Environmental Etiologic Theories." *Advances in Behavioral Pediatrics* 1 (1980): 29–51.

Lynch, Margaret. "The Prognosis of Child Abuse." *Journal of Child Psychology and Psychiatry* 19 (April 1978): 175–180.

Martin, Harold P. *The Abused Child.* Cambridge, MA: Ballinger Publishing Company, 1976.

Martin, Harold P., and Beezley, Patricia. "Behavioral Observations of Abused Children." *Developmental Medicine and Child Neurology* 19 (June 1977): 373–387.

Quinton, D., and Rutter, Michael. "Early Hospital Admissions and Later Disturbances of Behavior: An Attempted Replication of Douglas's Findings." *Developmental Medicine and Child Neurology* 18 (August 1976): 447–459.

Relich, Rosemarie; Giblin, Paul T.; Starr, Raymond H.; and Agronow, Samuel J. "Motor and Social Behavior in Abused and Control Children: Observation of Parent-Child Interactions." *Journal of Psychology* 106 (1980): 193–204.

Rutter, Michael. "Protective Factors in Children's Responses To Stress and Disadvantage," in *Primary Prevention of Psychopathology*, edited by M. W. Kent and J. Rolf. Hanover, NH: University Press of New England, 1979.

Rutter, Michael, and Quinton D. "Psychiatric Disorder: Ecological Factors and Concepts of Causation," in *Ecological Factors in Human Development*, edited by H. McGurk. Amsterdam, Holland: North-Holland, 1977.

Sandgrund, Alice; Gaines, Richard W.; and Green, Arthur H. "Child Abuse and Mental Retardation: A Problem of Cause and Effect." *American Journal of Mental Deficiency* 79 (November 1974): 327–330.

Toro, Paul A. "Developmental Effects of Child Abuse: A Review." *Child Abuse and Neglect* 6, 4 (1982): 423–431.

Yates, Alayne. "Narcissistic Traits in Certain Abused Children." *American Journal of Orthopsychiatry* 51 (January 1981): 55–62.

Sexual Abuse Prevention for Preschoolers:
A Pilot Program*

Joyce Borkin
Lesley Frank

The National Center on Child Abuse and Neglect [1983] estimated that as many as 500,000 children would be sexually abused in 1984. Studies reveal that one of every four female children will be sexually molested in some way before she is 18 years old, and one of every 20 children will be the victim of incest. The vast majority of the offenders, about 85%, are well known to the child victim [Walters 1975]. These people are often those whom the children have been taught to respect and obey, such as parents, relatives, teachers, and caretakers.

It appears that children are most vulnerable in their own homes. Research estimates indicate that 250,000 children are sexually molested by close relatives every year and that 2 million American families are involved in incest [James and Meyerding 1977; Stark 1984]. Increasingly, we hear reports of sexual abuse of very young children occurring in day care centers and nursery schools where caretakers use their positions of power with the children to convince them that the sexual activity is acceptable or to scare them into silence. The actual incidence of incest and sexual abuse of children can only be estimated because of the infrequency with which these offenses have been reported. We do know that child sexual abuse occurs with very young children and even infants, boys as well as girls, and at all levels of socioeconomic status and educational backgrounds [Lieske 1981; Stark 1984].

The long-term effects of sexual abuse on children have been studied with increasing concern in recent years. Sgroi [1982] has reported that some of the long-term effects include loss of self-esteem, inability to form constructive interpersonal relationships, and self-destructive behavior patterns. Groth [1980] reports evidence that seems to indicate that sexually abused children are at high risk of becoming sexually abusive adults. In a study of prisoners and mental health patients, he found that 81% had been sexually abused as children.

Sexual abuse and incest are "new" problems in that they are now being discussed and programs are being developed to help both the victims and the victimizers. Stories about sexual abuse and incest appear in the popular media: "Something About Amelia" on ABC TV (January 9, 1984) and the cover story of *Newsweek* (May 14, 1984) are examples. This coverage has increased the likelihood that

*Reprinted by special permission of the Child Welfare League of America from *Child Welfare*, vol. 65, no. 1, January–February 1986, pp. 75–82.

many people will accept information and discussion about these issues. Prevention programs that require the active participation of the target population can only be successful when the need or potential need for them is perceived. The time is ripe to educate parents about the dangers and to inform children about ways to protect themselves. Parents and teachers are beginning to ask for and accept information that will help them deal with these issues with their children. Social workers and other professionals in a variety of settings are in positions to initiate and promote programs aimed at helping children avoid sexual abuse. Although programs for elementary school children are available in many parts of the country, few have been developed for children under age 6, despite the data that show that very young children too are likely to be victims of sexual abuse [Kansas Committee for the Prevention of Child Abuse 1983; National Center on Child Abuse and Neglect 1983].*

Described here is a pilot project carried out during the 1983–1984 school year and aimed at the primary prevention and early detection of child abuse among preschool children. It was conducted in one day care center and three nursery schools in the greater Cincinnati metropolitan area (total number of children was 100). Its principal goals were to provide young children with the ability to protect themselves from sexual abuse by giving them an understanding of the difference between appropriate and inappropriate touching and instructions about what to do if someone touches them in an inappropriate way. Secondary goals were to provide parents and teachers with increased information about sexual abuse of very young children and to provide them with models and suggestions for discussions with children.

Program Description

Several sources were used to help construct the puppet show program used in this study. The "Bubbylonian Encounter," by Gene Mackey, is a three-character play intended for elementary school children that has been used for the past four years, first in Kansas City and then in various cities throughout the U.S. [Kansas Committee for the Prevention of Child Abuse 1983]. This presentation and other sources such as Dayee [1982] and Sanford [1980] stress the need to address four points when educating children about sexual abuse:

1. The establishment of the concept of private areas of the body that the children have a right to control, and the difference between touching that is "okay" and touching that is "not okay."

2. The permission and right to say "no" to an adult who is doing something wrong.

3. The importance of trusting one's own feelings; if something feels wrong, it probably is wrong.

---

*Cincinnati Children's Hospital Annual Report for 1983 states that 290 children were treated by the hospital for sexual abuse. The average age was 7 years, and 50% of the cases involved incest. Forty percent were 5 years old or younger, and 47% were under the age of 6.

4. The need to tell someone if touched inappropriately, and to keep telling until someone believes the report.

As the result of the theatrical program conducted for elementary school children in Kansas City, Kansas, there was a 200% increase in reports by children of inappropriate touching by adults. This increase in child-reported sexual abuse is stimulating an increase in interventions by medical and social work professionals [Kansas Committee for the Prevention of Child Abuse 1983].

The puppet show was created from materials attractive and familiar to young children to communicate information that enables children to take action for their own safety. Two adults use two familiar hand puppets to engage the preschoolers' attention and instruct them about inappropriate touching. The hand puppets are "Ernie," a character from the popular "Sesame Street" television program, and "Miss Piggy," one of the most popular Muppet characters. The adult performers hold the puppets out in full view of the children and interact with the puppets and the children in the audience as the play proceeds.

First Ernie and one adult performer discuss safety rules with each other and the audience, then they introduce the concept of sexual abuse as an event that requires safety rules. At this point the children are introduced to the concept of good touching. Examples of appropriate touching are demonstrated by the puppets, along with the explanation that good touching is something that makes you feel good. Then there is a discussion of the concept of "private parts" of the body, those parts that are covered by a bathing suit or underwear. These areas of their bodies are established as areas that the children themselves have the right to control, and they are instructed that no one has the right to touch those parts of them without a good reason. They are told that most people wouldn't want to touch them in a way that is not okay, but that inappropriate touching can come from a stranger or from someone they know well.

Through demonstration, the children are given rules to follow if someone tries to touch a private part of them without a good reason, or if anyone touches them in a way that makes them feel uneasy or confused. First they are told to say "no" very emphatically and to run away if they need to. Next they are instructed to tell an adult about any incident of "not okay" touching by an adult. Several examples of appropriate adults to tell are discussed, and the children are encouraged to join in and make suggestions.

As the puppet show ends, Miss Piggy and Ernie invite everyone to join them in some coloring activities, and the children are given a coloring page depicting the puppets. Each page has a "Scratch and Sniff" sticker in the corner—a colorful picture of an item such as grape jelly or strawberry soda, which when scratched smells like its illustration. The stickers are familiar to and enjoyed by preschoolers and are used here as a memory aid. During the coloring period the puppeteers interact with the children further and use this time to reinforce the messages and warnings of the puppet show.

Since a major objective of teaching children about inappropriate touch is to increase reports to adults of sexual approaches, it is necessary to educate the adults who may hear these reports so that they can respond appropriately to abused children and take proper action. A teacher-parent information session is offered in conjunction with the performance of the puppet show. Parents are invited to attend the performance with their children, and parents and teachers are given a pamphlet that outlines suggestions for discussing the subject of sexual abuse with children, ways to detect sexual abuse, and what to do if sexual abuse is suspected or reported to them by children. The adults who attend the performances are asked to complete brief evaluations.

Four to six weeks after the presentation of the puppet show, one of the participants returns to the site with more of the coloring pages and stickers. The children are again invited to color the picture of Ernie and Miss Piggy, and as they are coloring they are asked what they remember about the puppet show, specifically if they remember what to do if they are touched in an inappropriate way. The twofold purpose of this activity is to determine what information the children have retained from the puppet show and to reinforce the material covered in the performance.

Results of Follow-up with the Children

The follow-up questions were designed to see how many of the children had retained the basic information about what to do when somebody touched them in a "not okay" way. Children were scored as correct who said either "say no," or "run away," or "tell someone" in response to the question, "What should you do if someone tries to touch you in a way that doesn't feel good?" Children who said nothing or gave some incorrect response were scored as incorrect and reminded of the "rules."

The 83 children in the follow-up study were from programs in 4 different preschools. They were divided almost equally into 3 age groups: 25 were 3-year-olds, 30 were 4-year-olds, and 28 were 5-year-olds. Only one 3-year-old (4%) spontaneously offered one of the rules, while 13 (43%) of the 4-year-olds and 12 (43%) of the 5-year-olds did. The 3-year-olds clearly did less well on this performance test. This difference is statistically significant: Chi Square = 12.41, df = 2, $P < .01$.

These data would seem to imply that the 3-year-olds were too young to comprehend and remember the message of the puppet show. This indeed may be the case. It should be said, however, that the 3-year-olds by virtue of their age have had less experience in day care centers and nursery schools and may have been more reticent about responding to a virtual stranger than the older children were.

Adult Reactions to Presentation

At each presentation teachers and parents were asked for written comments and to rate the presentation (on a 1-to-5 scale, from "very well" to "not well") on four items: (1) how well it taught the concept of "not okay" touching; (2) how well it taught the concept of good touching; (3) how well it taught what to do if touched in an inappropriate way; and (4) how suitable the presentation was for this age group. In all, 25 adults responded to this questionnaire. Nineteen (76%) of the adults thought that the presentation did "very well" in teaching the rules for what to do if touched, and 18 (72%) believed that the presentation was very well suited to preschoolers. Fewer adults rated the performance as succeeding very well in teaching the concepts of good and bad touching: 13 (52%) and 14 (56%), respectively. These differences were not statistically significant, and 86% of the ratings overall were in the two highest categories on the scale.

Summary and Discussion

The program and follow-up procedures for the prevention and early detection of child sexual abuse described here can be inexpensively and easily implemented by social workers, teachers, and others who have contact with groups of young children. In this pilot effort the sample of preschool programs was selected "accidentally" from among those who requested the puppet show. No information is currently available on whether teachers in the four programs were more likely to be told about incidents or whether reports have been received by Child Protective Services as a result of the presentations. A controlled study is planned to determine whether there is an increased rate of reporting incidents of child sexual abuse from teachers or families who have been exposed to the program for preschoolers. Studies of this type would, of course, need to secure the cooperation of the child protective agency involved.

This study demonstrated that 3-, 4-, and 5-year-olds could attend to a puppet show about sexual abuse, although it would appear that only the 4- and 5-year-olds remembered the rules to any extent after 4 to 6 weeks. It was hoped that the "scratch and sniff" stickers and the coloring page would serve as prompts to remind the children of the rules and to reinforce them. A second or third follow-up would be needed to determine whether these reminder sessions actually produced any more learning. Continuous reinforcement of the concepts might be more effective. This might be achieved by giving each teacher a poster depicting the characters in the play that the children can decorate with paints, markers, or crayon. The poster can be hung on the wall and referred to periodically as a reminder.

At this point in the development of these types of programs we recommend the use of puppets, since everyone involved believed that they were effective in holding the children's attention and that they facilitated the presentation of the material involved at a level appropriate to this age group. We also recommend an increased emphasis on the concepts of good and bad touching, possibly by following the puppet show with vignettes or informal role plays involving the children, during which they are asked to determine whether the touching is appropriate or inappropriate. Finally, we hope to see a number of controlled studies to help determine whether children who have been exposed to a sexual abuse prevention program are more likely to report incidents of attempted molestation than those who have not.

It is extremely difficult if not impossible to evaluate accurately the success of the primary prevention aspects of this sort of program. We can measure the extent to which the children learn what to do and when to do it through testing and role play; we can survey parents as part of the follow-up to see whether there has been discussion of these topics and whether the child has told them of any attempted incidents. These data can be compared to those of control groups to determine if the program has had the desired effects in terms of increasing awareness of children and parents. However, the extent to which the children may actually ward off potential abusers is not measurable: first, because we do not have any truly accurate measure of the number of children in this age group who are currently abused; and second, because there is no way to collect accurate data on anything short of *reported* sexual abuse.

References

Dayee, Frances. *Private Zone: A Book Teaching Children Sexual Assault Prevention Tools*. Edmonds, WA: Franklin Press, 1982.

Groth, Nicholas. *Men Who Rape*. New York, NY: Decoba Press, 1980.

James, Jennifer, and Meyerding, Jane. "Early Sexual Experiences as a Factor in Prostitution." *American Journal of Psychiatry* 134 (December 1977): 1,381–1,385.

Kansas Committee for the Prevention of Child Abuse. *Conference Committee Report*, 1983.

Lieske, Anna Marie. "Incest: An Overview." *Perspectives in Psychiatric Care* 19 (March/April 1981).

National Center on Child Abuse and Neglect. "Understanding Child Sexual Abuse." *Annual Report*, 1983.

Sanford, Linda. *The Silent Children: A Parent's Guide to the Prevention of Child Sexual Abuse*. New York, NY: Doubleday and Co., 1980.

Sgroi, Suzanne. *Handbook of Clinical Intervention in Child Sexual Abuse*. Lexington, MA: Lexington Books, 1982.

Stark, Elizabeth. "The Unspeakable Family Secret." *Psychology Today* (May 1984).

Walters, David. *Physical and Sexual Abuse of Children*. Bloomington, IN: Indiana University Press, 1975.

Appendix C

Who Reports*

States and Territories	"Any Person" or "Any Other Person"**	Physician	Nurse	Surgeon	Osteopath	Dentist	Resident	Intern	Hospital/Institution Personnel	Practitioner of Healing Arts	Chiropractor	Optometrist	Podiatrist	Pharmacist	Mental Health Professional	Coroner/Medical Examiner
Alabama		X	X	X	X	X			X		X	X	X	X	X	X
Alaska		X	X	X	X	X			X	X	X	X			X	
Arizona		X	X	X	X	X	X	X			X		X		X	X
Arkansas		X	X	X	X	X	X	X	X						X	X
California		X	X	X		X	X	X	X	X	X		X			
Colorado		X	X	X	X	X		X	X		X		X		X	X
Connecticut	X	X	X	X	X	X	X	X			X	X	X		X	X
Delaware	X	X	X		X	X	X	X		X					X	X
District of Columbia		X	X			X						X			X	X
Florida	X	X	X													
Georgia		X	X		X	X	X	X					X		X	
Hawaii		X	X		X	X				X						X
Idaho	X	X	X				X	X								X
Illinois		X	X	X	X	X			X		X		X			X
Indiana	X															
Iowa		X	X	X	X	X	X	X	X	X	X	X	X		X	
Kansas			X			X	X	X		X					X	
Kentucky	X	X	X			X	X	X	X		X	X			X	X
Louisiana	X	X	X				X	X								
Maine		X	X		X	X	X	X			X		X		X	X
Maryland		X	X	X		X	X	X		X					X	
Massachusetts		X	X			X		X								X
Michigan		X	X			X										X
Minnesota									X	X					X	
Mississippi		X	X			X	X	X							X	
Missouri		X	X			X	X	X	X	X	X	X	X		X	X
Montana	X	X	X													
Nebraska	X	X	X						X							
Nevada		X	X	X	X	X	X	X	X		X	X			X	
New Hampshire	X	X	X	X	X	X	X	X	X		X	X			X	X
New Jersey	X															
New Mexico	X	X	X				X	X								
New York		X	X	X	X	X	X	X			X	X	X		X	X
North Carolina	X	X	X	X	X	X	X	X			X	X	X		X	X
North Dakota		X	X			X							X		X	X
Ohio		X	X	X		X	X	X					X		X	X
Oklahoma	X	X	X	X	X	X	X	X								
Oregon		X	X			X	X	X			X	X			X	
Pennsylvania		X	X		X	X			X	X	X	X	X		X	X
Rhode Island	X															
South Carolina		X	X			X					X		X		X	X
South Dakota		X	X	X	X	X	X	X			X	X	X		X	X
Tennessee	X															
Texas	X															
Utah	X		X													
Vermont		X	X	X	X	X	X	X	X		X					X
Virginia			X				X	X			X				X	
Washington		X	X	X	X	X					X	X	X	X	X	
West Virginia						X									X	
Wisconsin		X	X	X		X			X		X	X			X	X
Wyoming	X															
America Samoa		X	X	X	X	X	X	X	X		X	X	X		X	X
Guam		X	X	X		X		X	X	X	X	X	X		X	X
Puerto Rico	X	X	X			X	X	X	X	X	X			X		
Virgin Islands		X	X			X			X						X	

*Adapted from *Child Abuse and Neglect State Reporting Laws.* Washington, D.C.: NCCAN, Children's Bureau, 1979.

**A state that does not specify categories of professionals that must report, but instead requires that every person or any person report, is checked only in this column.

Who Reports

	WHO MUST REPORT												WHO MAY REPORT	
Teachers	Other School Personnel	Social Services Worker	Law Enforcement Officer	Peace Officer	Police Officers	Probation Officer	Parole Officer	Religious Healing Practitioner	Child Care Institution/Worker	Clergyman	Attorney	Others	States and Territories	Permissive Reporting
X	X	X	X	X					X			X	Alabama	●
X	†	X		X				X				X	Alaska	●
X	X	X		X								X	Arizona	
X	X	X	X	X					X				Arkansas	●
X	X	X		X		X		X	X	X		X	California	●
X	X	X						X	X			X	Colorado	●
X	X	X			X				X	X			Connecticut	
X	X	X											Delaware	
X	X	X	X						X				District of Columbia	●
X	†	X										X	Florida	
X	X	X	X						X				Georgia	●
X	†	X											Hawaii	●
X	†	X							X				Idaho	
X	X	X	X					X	X			X	Illinois	●
†	†												Indiana	
X	X	X		X					X				Iowa	
X	X	X	X										Kansas	●
X	X	X		X					X			X	Kentucky	
X	†	X										X	Louisiana	●
X	X	X	X					X					Maine	●
X	X	X	X		X	X	X					X	Maryland	
X	X	X			X	X						X	Massachusetts	●
X	X	X	X						X			X	Michigan	●
X	X	X	X						X				Minnesota	●
X	X	X	X						X	X			Mississippi	
X	X	X	X	X		X	X	X	X	X		X	Missouri	●
X	†	X	X								X		Montana	
X	X	X											Nebraska	
X	X	X						X	X	X			Nevada	●
X	X	X	X					X	X	X		X	New Hampshire	
†	†												New Jersey	
X	†	X	X										New Mexico	
†	X	X	X	X					X	X			New York	●
X	X	X	X						X			X	North Carolina	
X	X	X	X		X				X			X	North Dakota	●
X	X	X						X	X		X	X	Ohio	●
†	†												Oklahoma	
X	X	X		X					X	X	X	X	Oregon	
X	X	X	X	X					X	X		X	Pennsylvania	●
†	†												Rhode Island	
X	X	X	X		X				X	X			South Carolina	●
X	X	X	X										South Dakota	●
†	†												Tennessee	
†	†												Texas	
†	†												Utah	
†	†			X								X	Vermont	●
X	X	X	X			X			X	X		X	Virginia	●
X	X	X						X	X			X	Washington	●
X	X	X	X	X				X	X			X	West Virginia	●
X	X	X	X		X				X				Wisconsin	●
†	†												Wyoming	
X	X	X	X	X					X	X			America Samoa	●
X	X	X	X	X					X	X		X	Guam	
X	X	X							X				Puerto Rico	
X	X	X	X	X					X			X	Virgin Islands	●

†Teachers and other school personnel are required to report by state mandate of "any person" or "any other person" or "others."

Appendix D

Where to Find Reporting Information*

Since the responsibility for investigating reports of suspected child abuse and neglect lies at the state level, each state has established a child protective service reporting system. NCCAN annually compiles the descriptions of the reporting procedures in each state. Listed below are the names and addresses of the child protective services agency in each state, followed by the procedures for reporting suspected child maltreatment.

Alabama:
Alabama Department of Pensions and Security
Bureau of Family and Children's Services
64 North Union Street
Montgomery, AL 36130-1801

Reports made to county 24-hour emergency telephone services.

Alaska:
Department of Health and Social Services
Division of Family and Youth Services
Pouch H-05
Juneau, AK 99801

Reports made to Division of Social Services field offices.

American Samoa:
Government of American Samoa
Office of the Attorney General
Pago Pago, AS 96799

Reports made to the Department of Medical Services.

Arizona:
Department of Economic Security
P.O. Box 6123
Site COE 940A
Phoenix, AZ 85005

Reports made to Department of Economic Security local offices.

Arkansas:
Arkansas Department of Human Services
Division of Social Services
P.O. Box 1437
Little Rock, AR 72203

Reports made to the state-wide toll-free hotline (800) 482-5964.

California:
Office of Child Abuse Prevention
Department of Social Services
714-744 P Street
Sacramento, CA 95814

Reports made to County Departments of Welfare and Central Registry of Child Abuse (916) 455-7546, maintained by the Department of Justice.

---

*From "Child Abuse and Neglect: An Informed Approach to a Shared Concern." Washington, D.C.: Clearinghouse on Child Abuse and Neglect, 1986.

Colorado:
Department of Social
Services
1675 Sherman Street
Denver, CO 80203

Reports made to County Departments of Social Services.

Connecticut:
Connecticut Department of
Children and Youth Services
Child Protective Services
Department
Division of Children and
Youth Services
170 Sigourney Street
Hartford, CT 06105

Reports made to
(800) 842-2288

Delaware:
Delaware Department of
Health and Social Services
Division of Child Protective
Services
P.O. Box 309
Wilmington, DE 19899

Reports made to statewide
toll-free reporting hotline
(800) 292-9582.

District of Columbia:
District of Columbia Department of Human Services
Commission on Social
Services
Family Services
Administration
Child Protective Services
Division
First and I Streets, SW
Washington, DC 20024

Reports made to
(202) 727-0995

Florida:
Florida Child Abuse Registry
Central Admissions and
Interstate
1317 Winewood Boulevard
Tallahassee, FL 32301

Reports made to (800) 342-9152 or (904) 487-2625.

Georgia:
Georgia Department of Human Resources
Division of Family and Children Services
878 Peachtree Street, NE
Atlanta, GA 30309

Reports made to County Departments of Family and Children Services.

Guam:
Department of Public Health
and Social Services
Child Welfare Services
Child Protective Services
P.O. Box 2816
Agana, GU 96910

Reports made to the State
Child Protective Services
Agency at 646-8417.

Hawaii:
Department of Social Services and Housing
Public Welfare Division
Family and Children's
Services
P.O. Box 339
Honolulu, HI 96809

Reports made to the hotline
operated by Kapiolani-Children's Medical Center on
Oahu, and to branch offices of
the Division of Hawaii, Maui,
Kauai, Molokai.

Idaho:
Department of Health and
Welfare
Child Protection Division of
Welfare
Statehouse
Boise, ID 83702

Reports made to Department
of Health and Welfare Regional Offices.

191

Illinois:
Illinois Department of Children and Family Services, Station 509
State Administrative Offices
One North Old State Capitol Plaza
Springfield, IL 62706

Reports made to
(800) 25-ABUSE.

Indiana:
Indiana Department of Public Welfare-Child Abuse and Neglect
Division of Child Welfare-Social Services
141 South Meridian Street, 6th Floor
Indianapolis, IN 46225

Reports made to County Departments of Public Welfare.

Iowa:
Iowa Department of Human Services
Division of Community Programs
Hoover State Office Building
Fifth Floor
Des Moines, IA 50319

Reports made to the legally mandated toll-free reporting hotline (800) 362-2178

Kansas:
Kansas Department of Social and Rehabilitation Services
Division of Social Services
Child Protection and Family Services Section
Smith-Wilson Building
2700 West Sixth Street
Topeka, KS 66606

Reports made to Department of Social and Rehabilitation Services Area Offices.

Kentucky:
Kentucky Department for Human Resources

275 East Main Street
Frankfort, KY 40621

Reports made to County Offices within 4 regions of the state.

Louisiana:
Louisiana Department of Health and Human Resources
Office of Human Development
Baton Rouge, LA 70804

Reports made to the parish protective service units.

Maine:
Maine Department of Human Services Protective Services
Human Services Building
Augusta, ME 04333

Reports made to Regional Office or to State Agency at
(800) 452-1999.

Maryland:
Maryland Department of Human Resources
Social Services Administration
300 West Preston Street
Baltimore, MD 21201

Reports made to County Department of Social Services or to local law enforcement agencies.

Massachusetts:
Massachusetts Department of Social Services
Protective Services
150 Causeway Street, 11th Floor
Boston, MA 02114

Reports made to Regional Offices.

Michigan:
Michigan Department of Social Services
Office of Children and Youth Services

Protective Services Division
300 South Capitol Avenue
Lansing, MI 48926

Reports made to County Departments of Social Welfare.

Minnesota:
Minnesota Department of
Public Welfare
Department of Social
Services
Centennial Office Building
St. Paul, MN 55155

Reports made to the County
Departments of Public
Welfare.

Mississippi:
Mississippi Department of
Public Welfare
Division of Social Services
P.O. Box 352
Jackson, MS 39216

Reports made to
(800) 222-8000.

Missouri:
Missouri Child Abuse and
Neglect Hotline
Missouri Department of Social Services
Division of Family Services
DFS, P.O. Box 88
Broadway Building
Jefferson City, MO 65103

Reports made to
(800) 392-3738.

Montana:
Department of Social and Rehabilitative Services
Social Services Bureau
P.O. Box 4210
Helena, MT 59601

Reports made to County
Departments.

Nebraska:
Nebraska Department of Social Services

301 Centennial Mall South
5th Floor
Lincoln, NE 68509

Reports made to local law enforcement agencies or to County Divisions of Public
Welfare.

Nevada:
Department of Human
Resources
Division of Welfare
251 Jeanell Drive, Capitol
Complex
Carson City, NV 89710

Reports made to Division of
Welfare local offices.

New Hampshire:
New Hampshire Department
of Health and Welfare
Division of Welfare
Bureau of Child and Family
Services
Hazen Drive
Concord, NH 03301

Reports made to Division of
Welfare District Offices

New Jersey:
New Jersey Division of Youth
and Family Services
P.O. Box 510
One South Montgomery
Street
Trenton, NJ 08625

Reports made to (800) 729-
8610. District Offices also
provide 24-hour telephone
services.

New Mexico:
New Mexico Department of
Human Services
P.O. Box 2348
Santa Fe, NM 87503

Reports made to County Social Services Offices or to
(800) 432-6217.

New York:
New York Division of Family
and Children Services
Department of Social
Services
Child Protective Services
40 North Pearl Street
Albany, NY 12243

Reports made to (800) 342-
3720 or to District Offices.

North Carolina:
North Carolina Department
of Human Resources
Division of Social Services
325 North Salisbury Street
Raleigh, NC 27611

Reports made to County Departments of Social Services.

North Dakota:
North Dakota Department of
Human Services
Social Services Division
Children and Family Services
Unit Child Abuse and Ne-
glect Program
Russel Building, Highway 83
North
Bismarck, ND 58505

Reports made to Board of Social Services Area Offices and
to 24-hour reporting services
provided by Human Services
Centers.

Ohio:
Ohio Department of Public
Welfare
Bureau of Child Protective
Services
30 East Broad Street
Columbus, OH 43215

Reports made to County Departments of Public Welfare.

Oklahoma:
Oklahoma Department of In-
stitutions, Social and Rehabilitative Services
Division of Child Welfare

P.O. Box 25352
Oklahoma City, OK 73125

Reports made to
(800) 522-3511.

Oregon:
Department of Human
Services
Children's Services Division
Protective Services
509 Public Services Building
Salem, OR 97310

Reports made to local Children's Services Division Offices and to (503) 378-3016.

Pennsylvania:
Pennsylvania Department of
Public Welfare
Office of Children, Youth and
Families
Bureau of Family and Com-
munity Programs
Child Line and Abuse
Registry
Lanco Lodge, P.O. 2675
Harrisburg, PA 17102

Reports made to the toll-free
CHILDLINE (800) 932-0313.

Puerto Rico:
Puerto Rico Department of
Social Services
Services to Families with
Children
P.O. Box 11398
Fernandez Juncos Station
Santurce, PR 00910

Reports made to local offices
or to the Department.

Rhode Island:
Rhode Island Department of
Children and Families
610 Mt. Pleasant Avenue,
Bldg #7
Providence, RI 02908

Reports made to state agency
child protective services unit
at (800) 662-5100 or to District Offices

South Carolina:
  South Carolina Department
    of Social Services
  1535 Confederate Avenue
  P.O. Box 1520
  Columbia, SC 29202

  Reports made to County Departments of Social Services.

South Dakota:
  Department of Social
    Services
  Office of Children, Youth and
    Family Services
  Richard F. Kneip Building
  Pierre, SD 57501

  Reports made to local offices.

Tennessee:
  Tennessee Department of
    Human Services
  Child Protective Services
  State Office Building, Room
    410
  Nashville, TN 37219

  Reports made to County Departments of Human Services.

Texas:
  Texas Department of Human
    Resources
  Protective Services for Children Branch
  P.O. Box 2960, MC 537-A
  Austin, TX 78769

  Reports made to
  (800) 252-5400.

Utah:
  Department of Social
    Services
  Division of Family Services
  P.O. Box 2500
  Salt Lake City, UT 84110

  Reports made to Division of
  Family Services District
  Offices.

Vermont:
  Vermont Department of Social and Rehabilitative
    Services

Division of Social Services
103 South Main Street
Waterbury, VT 05676

Reports made to state agency
at (800) 828-3422 or to District
Offices (24-hour services).

Virgin Islands:
  Virgin Islands Department of
    Social Welfare
  Division of Social Services
  P.O. Box 500
  Charlotte Amalie
  St. Thomas VI 00801

  Reports made to the Division
  of Social Services

Virginia:
  Virginia Department of
    Welfare
  Bureau of Family and Community Programs
  Blair Building
  8007 Discovery Drive
  Richmond, VA 23288

  Reports made to (800) 552-7096 in Virginia and (804) 281-9081 outside the state.

Washington:
  Department of Social and
    Health Services
  Community Services Division
  Child Protective Services
  Mail stop OB 41-D
  Olympia, WA 98504

  Reports made to local Social
  and Health Services Offices.

West Virginia:
  West Virginia Department of
    Human Services
  Division of Social Services
  Child Protective Services
  State Office Building
  1900 Washington Street East
  Charleston, WV 25305

  Reports made to
  (800) 352-6513.

Wisconsin:
  Wisconsin Department of
    Health and Social Services
  Division of Community
    Services
  Office of Children, Youth and
    Families
  1 West Wilson Street
  Madison, WI 53702

  Reports made to County Social Services Office.

Wyoming:
  Department of Health and
    Social Services
  Division of Public Assistance
    and Social Services
  Hathaway Building
  Cheyenne, WY 82002

  Reports made to County Departments of Public Assistance
  and Social Services.

Appendix E

National Organizations Concerned with Child Abuse and Neglect

The address of the National Center on Child Abuse and Neglect is

NCCAN
P.O. Box 1182
Washington, DC 20013

Other facilities of NCCAN include two national resource centers and a clearinghouse:

National Child Abuse Clinical Resource Center
Dr. Richard Krugman, Director
Kempe Center
University of Colorado
Health Sciences Center
1205 Oneida Street
Denver, CO 80220
(303) 321-3963

National Resource Center for Child Abuse and Neglect
Patricia Schene, Director
American Humane Association
American Association for Protecting Children
9725 East Hampden Avenue
Denver, CO 80231
(303) 695–0811

National Clearinghouse on Child Abuse and Neglect Research and Information

The Clearinghouse provides a number of services and products, including bibliographies, custom searches, annual reviews, in-depth analyses, compilations of resource materials, and directories. A fee is charged for certain services and products, such as data tapes, mailing labels, and copies of noncopyrighted materials.

For a current catalog of NCCAN publications available from the Clearinghouse, write to

NCCAN
Children's Bureau
Department of Health and Human Services
P.O. Box 1182
Washington, DC 20013

The list of organizations that follows is reprinted from "Child Abuse and Neglect: An Informed Approach to a Shared Concern" (NCCAN Clearinghouse, 1986).

Action for Child Protection
202 E Street, NW
Washington, DC 20002
(202) 393–1090
Contact: Diane DePanfilis

American Academy of
 Pediatrics
141 Northwest Point Road
P.O. Box 927
Elk Grove Village, IL 60007
(800) 433–9016, ext. 7937
Contact: James Harisiades

American Bar Association
National Legal Resource
 Center for Child Advocacy
 and Protection
1800 M Street, NW, Suite 200
Washington, DC 20036
(202) 331–2250
Professional and institutional
 inquiries only.

American Humane Association
American Association for
 Protecting Children
9725 East Hampden Avenue
Denver, CO 80231
(303) 695–0811
Contact: Kathryn Bond

American Medical Association
Health and Human Behavior
 Department
535 North Dearborn
Chicago, IL 60610
(312) 645–4523

American Public Welfare
 Association
1125 15th Street, NW, Suite 300
Washington, DC 20005
Contact: A. Sidney Johnson III,
          Executive Director

Association of Junior Leagues
825 Third Avenue
New York, NY 10022
(212) 355–4380
Contact: For legislative informa-
         tion, Sally Orr, Public Poli-
         cy Unit

Re: local chapter CAN
programs, Lisa Farrell

Boys Clubs of America
611 Rockville Pike, Suite 230
Rockville, MD 20852
(301) 251–6676
Contact: Robbie Callaway

C. Henry Kempe Center for
 Prevention and Treatment of
 Child Abuse and Neglect
1025 Oneida Street
Denver, CO 80220
(303) 321–3963
Contact: Gail Ryan (for bookstore
         and publications)

Child Welfare League of America
440 First Street, NW, Suite 310
Washington, DC 20001
(202) 638–2952

Childhelp USA
6463 Independence Avenue
Woodland Hills, CA 91367
Hotline: 1-800-FOR-A-CHILD
         (367–2–24453)

General Federation of
 Women's Clubs
1734 N Street, NW
Washington, DC 20036
(202) 347–3168
Contact: Legislative Office

Institute for the Community as
 Extended Family (ICEF)
P.O. Box 952
San Jose, CA 95108
(408) 280–5055

National Association of Social
 Workers
7981 Eastern Avenue
Silver Spring, MD 20910
(301) 565–0333
Contact: Leila Whiting

National Black Child
 Development Institute
1463 Rhode Island Avenue, NW
Washington, DC 20005
(202) 387–1281

National Center for Child Abuse
and Neglect (NCCAN)
Children's Bureau
Administration for Children,
Youth and Families
Office of Human Development
Services
Department of Health and
Human Services
P.O. Box 1182
Washington, DC 20013
(301) 251-5157–Clearinghouse

National Center for Missing and
Exploited Children
Education, Prevention, and
Public Awareness Division
1835 K Street, NW, Suite 700
Washington, DC 20006
(202) 634-9821

National Committee for
Prevention of Child Abuse
332 South Michigan Avenue
Chicago, IL 60604

National Council of Jewish
Women
Children and Youth Priority,
Program Department
15 East 26th Street
New York, NY 10010
(212) 532-1740

National Council of Juvenile
and Family Court Judges
P.O. Box 8978
Reno, NV 89507
(702) 784-6012
Contact: James Toner

National Council on Child
Abuse and Family Violence
1050 Connecticut Ave., NW
Suite 300
Washington, DC 20036
1-800-222-2000
Contact: Mary-Ellen Rood

National Crime Prevention
Council
733 15th Street, NW, Room 540
Washington, DC 20005

(202) 393-7141
Contact: Allie Bird, Director of
Public Information

National Education Association
Human and Civil Rights Unit
1201 16th Street, NW
Room 714
Washington, DC 20036
(202) 822-7711
Contact: Mary Faber

National Exchange Club
Foundation for Prevention of
Child Abuse
3050 Central Avenue
Toledo, OH 43606
(419) 535-3232
Contact: George Mezinko, Director
of Foundation Services

National Network of Runaway
and Youth Services
905 6th Street, NW, Suite 411
Washington, DC 20024
(202) 488-0739
Contact: Renee Woodworth

Parents Anonymous
7120 Franklin Avenue
Los Angeles, CA 90046
800-421-0353 (toll-free)
(213) 876-9642 (business phone)
Contact: Margot Fritz, Acting
Executive Director

Parents United/Daughters and
Sons United/Adults Molested as
Children United
P.O. Box 952
San Jose, CA 95108
(408) 280-5055

SCAN Associates
P.O. Box 7445
Little Rock, AK 72217
1-800-482-5850, ext. 1310–in
Arkansas only
(501) 661-1774–outside State
Contact: Norma Smothers,
Training Director

Appendix F

Immunity*

States and Territories	Civil and Criminal Immunity in Making of a Report	Immunity for the Taking of Photographs	Immunity for the Taking of X-rays	Immunity in Resulting Judicial Proceedings	Requirement of Good Faith	Good Faith Presumed
Alabama	X			X		
Alaska	X			X	X	
Arizona	X			X	X	
Arkansas	X	X				X
California	X			X	X	
Colorado	X	X	X	X		X
Connecticut	X			X	X	
Delaware	X			X	X	
District of Columbia	X			X	X	X
Florida	X	X	X	X		X
Georgia	X			X	X	
Hawaii	X			X	X	
Idaho	X			X	X	
Illinois	X	X	X	X		X
Indiana	X	X	X	X	X	X
Iowa	X			X	X	
Kansas	X			X	X	
Kentucky	X			X		
Louisiana	X			X	X	
Maine	X			X		X
Maryland	X			X	X	
Massachusetts	X				X	
Michigan	X	X	X			X
Minnesota	X				X	
Mississippi	X			X		X
Missouri	X	X	X	X	X	
Montana	X			X		X
Nebraska	X			X	X	
Nevada	X			X	X	
New Hampshire	X			X	X	
New Jersey	X			X	X	
New Mexico	X			X		X
New York	X	X				X
North Carolina	X			X	X	
North Dakota	X			X		X
Ohio	X			X		
Oklahoma	X			X ♦	X ♦	
Oregon	X			X	X	
Pennsylvania	X	X		X	X	X
Rhode Island	X			X	X	
South Carolina	X			X	X	X
South Dakota	X			X	X	
Tennessee	X					X
Texas	X			X	X	
Utah	X	X	X	X		
Vermont	X			X	X	
Virginia	X			X	X	
Washington	X			X	X	
West Virginia	X	X	X	X		
Wisconsin	X	X			X	X
Wyoming	X	X	X		X	X
America Samoa	X	X			X	X
Guam	X	X		X	X	X
Puerto Rico	X					
Virgin Islands	X	X	X		X	

*From *Child Abuse and Neglect State Reporting Laws.* Washington, D.C.: NCCAN, Children's Bureau, 1979.

Appendix G

Reporting Procedure*

States and Territories	Orally, Followed By Writing	Time When Writing is Due	As Soon As Possible (ASAP) or Not Specified (NS)	Orally Only	Orally or In Writing	Orally, Then In Writing If Requested	Time When Due, If Requested	Procedure Not Specified	Receipt of Report Social Services Agency	Law Enforcement Agency	Other Agency
Alabama	X		NS						X	X	X
Alaska								X	X		
Arizona								X	X	X	
Arkansas						X	48 hours		X		
California	X	36 hours							X	X	X
Colorado	X		NS						X	X	
Connecticut	X	72 hours							X	X	
Delaware						X	NS		X		
District of Columbia						X	NS		X	X	
Florida	X		ASAP						X		
Georgia						X	NS		X		
Hawaii	X		ASAP						X		
Idaho								X		X	
Illinois	X	24 hours							X		
Indiana				X					X	X	
Iowa	X	48 hours							X		
Kansas						X	NS				X
Kentucky						X	48 hours		X		
Louisiana	X	5 days							X	X	
Maine						X	48 hours		X		
Maryland	X	48 hours							X	X	
Massachusetts	X	48 hours							X		
Michigan	X	72 hours							X		
Minnesota	X		ASAP						X	X	
Mississippi	X		ASAP						X		
Missouri	X	48 hours							X		
Montana								X	X		X
Nebraska	X		NS							X	
Nevada	X		ASAP						X	X	X
New Hampshire						X	48 hours		X		
New Jersey								X	X		
New Mexico								X	X		X
New York	X	48 hours							X		X
North Carolina				X					X		
North Dakota				X		X	48 hours		X		
Ohio						X	NS		X	X	X
Oklahoma	X		ASAP						X		
Oregon				X					X	X	
Pennsylvania	X	48 hours							X		
Rhode Island	X		NS						X		
South Carolina				X					X	X	
South Dakota				X					X		X
Tennessee								X	X	X	X
Texas	X	5 days							X	X	X
Utah						X	48 hours		X	X	
Vermont	X	7 days							X		
Virginia	X		NS						X		
Washington						X	NS		X	X	
West Virginia						X	48 hours		X		
Wisconsin						X	NS		X	X	
Wyoming						X	NS		X	X	
America Samoa						X	48 hours				X
Guam	X	48 hours							X		
Puerto Rico							48 hours		X		
Virgin Islands						X	48 hours				X

*From *Child Abuse and Neglect State Reporting Laws*. Washington, D.C.: NCCAN, Children's Bureau, 1979.

Appendix H

Sample Reporting Form*

REPORT OF CHILD(REN) ALLEGED TO BE SUFFERING FROM SERIOUS PHYSICAL OR EMOTIONAL INJURY BY ABUSE OR NEGLECT*

> Massachusetts law requires an individual who is a mandated reporter to **immediately** report any allegation of serious physical or emotional injury resulting from abuse or neglect to the Department of Social Services by oral communication. This written report must then be completed **within 48 hours** of making the oral report and should be sent to the appropriate Department office.

Please complete all sections of this form. If some data is unknown, please signify. If some data is uncertain, place a question mark after the entry.

DATA ON CHILDREN REPORTED:

	NAME	CURRENT LOCATION/ADDRESS	SEX	AGE OR DATE OF BIRTH
1)	Thomas Smythe, Jr.	195 East St., Westville, MA	☒ Male ☐ Female	10/09/72
2)			☐ Male ☐ Female	
3)			☐ Male ☐ Female	
4)			☐ Male ☐ Female	
5)			☐ Male ☐ Female	

DATA ON MALE GUARDIAN OR PARENT:

Name: Thomas (First)   Brown (Last)   (Middle)

Address: 195 East St. (Street and Number)   Westville (City/Town)   MA (State)

Telephone Number: 555-4567   Age: 40(?)

DATA ON FEMALE GUARDIAN OR PARENT:

Name: Gloria (First)   Brown (Last)   (Middle)

Address: 195 East St. (Street and Number)   Westville (City/Town)   MA (State)

Telephone Number: 555-4567   Age: 32

DATA ON REPORTER/REPORT:

10/12/83 (Date of Report)   ☒ Mandatory Report   ☐ Voluntary Report

Reporter's Name: Francine (First)   Garcia (Last) (teacher)

Reporter's Address: (If the reporter represents an institution, school, or facility please indicate.)

South Westville Middle School (Street)   Westville (City/Town)

MA (State)   (Zip Code)   555-3456 (Telephone Number)

Has reporter informed caretaker of report? ☐ YES ☒ NO

ABUSE/NEGLECT REPORT - 3   (Revised April, 1983)

---

*Form reprinted with permission of Massachusetts Department of Social Services. *Filled-in data is fictitious and used only as an example.*

What is the nature and extent of the injury, abuse, maltreatment or neglect, including prior evidence of same? (Please cite the source of this information if not observed first hand.)

Tom has become increasingly withdrawn this school year. He apparently has no friends, eats alone, and has been seen crying on several occasions. In addition, the boy's grades are deteriorating and he is in danger of failing all subjects. According to other teachers, last year he did well in school and had many friends. Also, the school nurse reports that Tom appears to be losing weight.

What are the circumstances under which the reporter became aware of the injuries, abuse, maltreatment or neglect?

I called Tom's mother who reported that Mr. Brown has recently returned from a temporary assignment in Germany (he works for an oil company). The couple has been arguing about Mr. Brown's methods of discipline, which Mrs. Brown thinks are too harsh. They include isolating Tom from his half-brothers and sisters (Tom is from an earlier marriage of Mrs. Brown). For days at a time the boy is locked in his room from the time he gets home from school in the afternoon until he goes to school the next morning.

What action has been taken thus far to treat, shelter or otherwise assist the child to deal with this situation?

In my conversation with Tom's mother, she said there was nothing she could do. A parent/teacher conference was requested with both parents, but they refused this request. Tom was referred to the guidance counselor.

Please give other information which you think might be helpful in establishing the cause of the injury and/or the person responsible for it. If known, please provide the name(s) of the alleged perpetrator(s).

Tom told the guidance counselor that on some days the only meal he gets is lunch at school.

I would like to be contacted by the social worker.

Francine Garcia
Signature of Reporter

ABUSE/NEGLECT REPORT - 3   (Revised April, 1983)

Appendix I

Resources

Note: For easier identification the following key has been established:

S = Sexual abuse
N = Neglect
P = Physical abuse
M = Miscellaneous maltreatment

Further Reading for Educators

Bakan, David. *Slaughter of Innocents: A Story of the Battered Child Phenomenon.* San Francisco: Jossey-Bass, 1971. (M)

Brenton, M. "What Can Be Done About Child Abuse." *Today's Education* (September-October 1977): 30–33.

Broadhurst, D. D. "Policy-Making: First Step for Schools in the Fight Against Child Abuse and Neglect." *Elementary School Guidance and Counseling* 10 (1976): 222–26.

_____. "Update: What Schools Are Doing About Child Abuse and Neglect." *Children Today* (January-February 1978): 22–24.

Butler, Sandra. *Conspiracy of Silence: The Trauma of Incest.* San Francisco: New Glide Publications, 1978. (S)

Caskey, O.L., and Richardson, F. "Understanding and Helping Child Abuse Parents." *Elementary School Guidance and Counseling* 9 (1975): 196–208.

Chase, Naomi Feigelson. *A Child Is Being Beaten: Violence Against Children, An American Tragedy.* New York: Holt, Rinehart and Winston, 1975. (M)

Child Abuse and Neglect Project. *Education Policies and Practices Regarding Child Abuse and Neglect and Recommendations for Policy Development.* Denver: Education Commission of the States. 1976. (M)

_____. *Teacher Education: An Active Participant in Solving the Problem of Child Abuse and Neglect.* Denver: Education Commission of the States, 1977. (M)

Child Abuse and Neglect: The Problem of Its Management. Vols. 1, 2, and 3. Washington, D.C.: U.S. Department of Health, Education and Welfare, 1975. (M)

Child Sexual Abuse: Incest, Assault and Sexual Exploitation. Washington, D.C.: U.S. Department of Health and Human Services, 1981. (S)

Child Welfare League of America. *Standards for Child Protective Services.* New York: Child Welfare League of America, 1973. (M)

Children Alone: What Can Be Done About Abuse and Neglect. Reston Va.: Council for Exceptional Children, 1977.

Davoren, E. "Foster Placement of Abused Children." *Children Today* 4, no. 2 (1975): 41. (P)

_____. "Working with Abusive Parents: A Social Worker's View." *Children Today* 4, no. 2 (1975): 38–43. (P)

DeFrancis, Vincent. *Protecting the Child Victim of Sex Crimes Committed by Adults*. Final Report. Denver: American Humane Association. Children's Division, 1969. (S)

Education Policies and Practices Regarding Child Abuse and Neglect and Recommendations for Policy Development. Denver: Education Commission of the States, 1976.

Finkelhor, David. *Sexually Victimized Children*. New York: MacMillan, 1979. (S)

Flomenhaft, K.; Machotka, Paul; Pittman, F. S. "Incest as a Family Affair." *Family Process* 6, no. 1: 98–116. (S)

Fontana, Vincent J. *Somewhere a Child Is Crying: Maltreatment, Causes and Prevention*. New York: Macmillan, 1973. (M)

Forward, S., and Buck, C. *Betrayal of Innocence: Incest and Its Devastation*. New York: Penguin Books, 1978. (S)

Fraser, Brian G. *The Educator and Child Abuse*. National Committee for Prevention of Child Abuse, Suite 510, 111 E. Wacker Dr., Chicago, IL 60601. (M)

Geiser, Robert. *Hidden Victims*. Boston: Beacon Press, 1979. (S)

Geiser, Robert L. *The Illusion of Caring: Children in Foster Care*. Boston: Beacon Press, 1973. (M)

Gil, David. *Violence Against Children*. Cambridge: Harvard University Press, 1970. (P)

Gil, David G. "What Schools Can Do About Child Abuse." *Childhood Education* 52, no. 2 (1975): 58–62. (M)

Groth, A. Nicholas. *Men Who Rape: The Psychology of the Offender*. New York: Plenum Press, 1979. (S)

Halperin, Michael. *Helping Maltreated Children: School and Community Involvement*. St. Louis: C. V. Mosby Co., 1979. (M)

Helfer, Ray E., and Kempe, C. Henry. *Child Abuse and Neglect: The Family and the Community*. Cambridge, Mass.: Ballinger, 1976. (M)

_____ and _____, eds., *The Battered Child*. Chicago: University of Chicago Press, 1974. (P)

Herman, Judith. *Father-Daughter Incest*. Cambridge, Mass.: Harvard University Press, 1981. (S)

Holmes, Sally A., and others. "Working with the Parents in Child Abuse Cases." *Social Casework* 56, no. 2 (1975): 3–12. (P)

Hopkins, J. "The Nurse and the Abused Child." *Nursing Clinics of North America* 5 (1970): 594. (P)

Jirsa, James. *Child Abuse and Neglect: A Handbook*. Madison Metropolitan School District, 545 W. Dayton St., Madison, WI 53703. (M)

Kadushin, A. *Child Welfare Services*. New York: Macmillan, 1974. (M)

Katz, Sanford N. *When Parents Fail: The Law's Response to Family Breakdown*. Boston: Beacon Press, 1971. (M)

Kempe, C. Henry, and Helfer, Ray E. *Helping the Battered Child and His Family*. Philadelphia: J. B. Lippincott Co., 1972. (M)

Kempe, R., and Kempe, C. *Child Abuse*. Cambridge, Mass.: Harvard University Press, 1978. (M)

Martin, H. P., ed. *The Abused Child: A Multi-Disciplinary Approach to Developmental Issues*. Cambridge, Mass.: Ballinger, 1976. (P)

Mulford, Robert. *Emotional Neglect of Children*. Denver: American Humane Association (P. O. Box 1266). (N)

Murdock, G. G. "The Abused Child and the School System." *Public Health* 60 (1970): 105. (P)

National Center on Child Abuse and Neglect. Child Abuse and Neglect. Audiovisual Materials. Washington, D.C.: U.S. Department of Health, Education and Welfare, 1977. (M)

Newberger, Eli H., and Daniel, Jessica H. "Knowledge and Epidemiology of Child Abuse: A Critical Review of Concepts." *Pediatric Annals* (March 1976). (P)

Open the Door on Child Abuse and Neglect: Prevention and Reporting Kit. Ohio Department of Public Welfare, Children's Protective Services, 30 East Broad St., Columbus, Ohio 43215. (M)

Polansky, N. A.; Borgman, R. D.; and Desaix, C. *Roots of Futility*. San Francisco: Jossey-Bass, 1972. (N)

Polansky, N. A., and others. "Isolation of the Neglectful Family." *American Journal of Orthopsychiatry* 49 (1979): 149-52. (N)

Polansky, N. A.; Holly, C.; and Polansky, N. F. *Profile of Neglect: A Survey of the State of Knowledge of Child Neglect*. Washington, D.C.: Department of Health, Education and Welfare, Community Services Administration, 1975. (N)

Red Horse, J. E., et al. "Family Behavior of Urban American Indians." *Social Casework* 59 (1978).

Rush, Florence. *The Best Kept Secret: Sexual Abuse of Children*. Englewood Cliffs, N.J.: Prentice-Hall, 1980. (S)

Schmitt, B. D. "What Teachers Need to Know About Child Abuse and Neglect." *Childhood Education* 52 (1975): 58-62. (M)

Schmitt, Barton D., ed. *The Child Protection Team Handbook*. New York: Garland S.T.P.M. Press, 1978. (M)

Sgroi, Suzanne M. "Molestation of Children: The Last Frontier in Child Abuse." *Children Today* 4 (1975): 18-21.

Sherman, E. A.; Neuman, R.; and Skyne, A. W. *Children Adrift in Foster Care*. New York. Child Welfare League of America, 1973. (M)

Soeffing M. "Abused Children Are Exceptional Children." *Exceptional Children* 42 (1975): 126-33.

Werner, Emmy E. "Cross-Cultural Child Development." *Children Today* (March/April 1979).

Pamphlets Published by U.S. Government Printing Office

American Indian Law: Relationship to Child Abuse and Neglect. 1981. 56 pp. HE 23.1210: In 2 S/N 017-092-0071-5

Child Abuse and Neglect: A Self-Instructional Text for Head Start Personnel. 1977. 135 pp. il. HE 23.1108:C 43 S/N 017-090-00035-6

Child Abuse and Neglect Among the Military: A Special Report from the National Center on Child Abuse and Neglect. 9 pp. HE 23.1210:M 59 S/N 017-092-0074-0

Child Abuse and Neglect Prevention and Treatment in Rural Communities: Two Approaches. 1978. 213 pp. il. HE 23.1210:C 73 S/N 017-090-0040-2

Child Abuse and Neglect, The Problem and Its Management: Volume 2, The Roles and Responsibilities of Professionals. 1976. HE 1.480:P 94/v.2 S/N 017-092-00017-1

Community Approach: The Child Protection Coordinating Committee. 1979. 82 pp. HE 23.1210/4:C 33 S/N 017-092-00040-5

Early Childhood Programs and the Prevention and Treatment of Child Abuse and Neglect: For Workers in Head Start, Family Day Care, Preschool and Day Care Programs. 1979. 76 pp. HE 23.12104/4: Ea 7 S/N 017-092-00044-8

Educator's Role in the Prevention and Treatment of Child Abuse and Neglect. 1979. 74 pp. HE 23.1210/4:Ed 8 S/N 017-092-00043-0

How to Plan and Carry Out a Successful Public Awareness Program on Child Abuse and Neglect. Rev. 1980. 71 pp. HE 23.1210/4:AW 1 S/N 017-092-0067-7

Interdisciplinary Glossary on Child Abuse and Neglect: Legal, Medical, Social Work Terms. Rev. 1980. 45 pp. il. HE 23.1210:G 51/980 S/N 017-092-0062-6

Planning and Implementing Child Abuse and Neglect Service Programs: The Experience of Eleven Demonstration Projects. 1977. 16 pp. il. HE 1.480:969 S/N 017-092-0023-5

Profile of Neglect: A Survey of the State of Knowledge of Child Neglect. 1975. 57 pp. HE 17.702:N 31 S/N 017-065-00006-8

Sexual Abuse of Children: Selected Readings. 1980. 193 pp. il. HE 23.1210:Se 9/2 S/N 017-090-00057-7

Parenting Skills Workshops

Responsive Parenting by Saf Lerman
American Guidance Service Publishers' Building
Circle Pines, MN 55014-1796
1-800-328-2560 (in Minnesota)
1-612-786-4343 (call collect)

Prevention Projects

Bridgework Theater
113-½ East Lincoln Avenue, Suite 3
Goshen, IN 46526
Carol Plummer, Project Director

Judith Little
Rt. 2, Box 330B
Mebane, NC 27302
(919) 563–1890
(for information on Trainer's Manual,
including fifth grade curriculum)

    OR

Alamana Caswell
Area Mental Health and Mental Retardation Project
Child and Youth Services
1946 Martin Street
Burlington, NC 27215
(for information on Parents' Booklet)

Illusion Theater
Hennepin Center for the Arts
528 Hennepin Avenue
Minneapolis, MN 55403
(612) 339–4944
Cordelia Kent, Director
Applied Theater

C. Henry Kempe National Center
for the Prevention and Treatment
of Child Abuse and Neglect
1205 Oneida Street
Denver, CO 80220
(for annotated list of audiovisual
library loan materials for educators and
school personnel, students, community
groups, child welfare professionals,
medical personnel, lay therapists)

Puppet Shows

What Should I Do? (S)
Elfin Productions
P.O. Box 422
Williamsburg, MA 01096

Video Puppet Productions (S)
Child Sexual Abuse Prevention Project
Franklin/Hampshire Community Mental Health Center
76 Pleasant Street
Northampton, MA 01060

Audiovisuals for Educators and Community Awareness

Child Abuse and the Law
Motion Picture Co., Inc. 1977
  27 min. film. Available from
Perennial Educ. Inc., 477 Roger Williams
P.O. Box 855 — Ravinia
Highland Park, IL 60035

Child Abuse: Cradle of Violence
Prod: Mitchell-Gebhardt Film Co.
  22 min. film. Available from
J. Gary Mitchell Film Co., Inc.
2000 Bridgeway
Sausalito, CA 94965

Child Abuse and Neglect: What the Educator Sees
  15 min. filmstrip and cassette. Available from
National Audio Visual Center, GSA Order Section
Washington, DC 20409

Children: A Case of Neglect
  56 min. film. Available from
Macmillan Films, Inc.
34 S. MacQueston Parkway
Mt. Vernon, NY 10550

Cipher in the Snow (Emotional abuse or neglect)
  23 min. film. Available from
Brigham Young University, Media Marketing
West Stadium
Provo, Utah 84602

Fragile, Handle with Care (looks at abuser)
Produced by KTAR-TV Productions
  26 min. film. Available from
High Court of Southern California
100 Border Avenue
Solan Beach, CA 92075

Incest: The Victim Nobody Believes
Produced by Mitchell-Gebhardt Film Co.
  21 min. film. Available from
J. Gary Mitchell Film Co., Inc.
2000 Bridgeway
Sausalito, CA 94965

*Lift a Finger: The Administrator's Role in Combating
Child Abuse and Neglect*
  12 min. slide & cassette. Available from
Education Professionals Development Consortium
1750 Seamist
Houston, TX 77008

The Sexually Abused Child
Cavalcade Productions, 1978
 10 min. film. Available from
Coronet/MTI
108 Wilmot Road
Deerfield, IL 60015

We Can Help. Unit 15, Specialized Training for Educators
 15 min. filmstrip & cassette
National Center on Child Abuse and Neglect
P.O. Box 1182
Washington, DC 20013

Whose Child Is This?
Shands (Alfred) Productions, Louisville, KY
 30 min. video cassette. Available from
Junior League of Louisville, Inc.
627 Main Street
Louisville, KY 40202

Books or Pamphlets to Use with Children

Adams C., and Fay, J. *No More Secrets*. San Luis Obispo, Calif.: Impact Publishing Co., 1981 (school age) (S)

Bassett, C. *My Very Own Special Body Book*. Redding, Calif.: Hawthorne Press, 1980. (school age) (S)

Dolan, Edward F. *Child Abuse*. New York: Franklin Watts, 1980. (high school) (M)

Fay, J. *He Told Me Not to Tell*. Renton, Wash.: King County Rape Relief, 1979. (school age) (S)

_____. *Good Touch, Bad Touch*. Norristown, Penna.: Rape Crisis Center of Montgomery County (P.O. Box 1179, 501 Swede St., Norristown, PA 19401). (S)

Haskins, James. *The Child Abuse Help Book*. Reading, Mass.: Addison Wesley Publishing Co., 1982. (junior high & high school) (M)

Hyde, Margaret O. *Cry Softly! The Story of Child Abuse*. Philadelphia: Westminster Press, 1980. (high school) (M)

Marshall, James. *George and Martha*. Boston: Houghton Mifflin, 1972. (school age) (S)

Sanford, L. *Come Tell Me Right Away: A Positive Approach to Warning Children About Sexual Abuse*. Fayetteville, N.Y.: Ed.-U Press, 1982. (school age) (S)

Stowell, J., and Diltzel, M. *My Very Own Book About Me*. Spokane, Wash.: Spokane Rape Crisis Network, 1981. (Lutheran Social Services of Washington, 1226 N. Howard, Spokane, WA 99201) (Teacher's guide available) (young children) (S)

Sweet, P. E. *Something Happened to Me*. Racine, Wis.: Mother Courage Press, 1981. (5-10 years) (S)

Williams, J. *Red Flag, Green Flag People*. Fargo, N.D.: Rape and Crisis Center, 1980. (P.O. Box 1655, Fargo, ND 58107) (5-9 years) (S)

Training Programs to Use With Children

Personal Safety Curriculum: Prevention of Child Sexual Abuse. Geri Crisci, P.O. Box 763, Hadley, MA 01035. (A unit to sensitize children in all grades toward prevention of and protection from sexual assault.)

Seattle Rape Relief Developmental Disabilities. 1825 South Jackson, Suite 102, Seattle, WA 98114. (Special education curriculum on sexual abuse designed for handicapped children.)

Sexual Abuse Prevention Program. Illusion Theatre, 528 Hennepin Avenue, Minneapolis, MN 55403. (Provides theater productions to use with children to protect from sexual abuse.)

Women Against Rape. Child Assault Prevention Project. P.O. Box 02084, Columbus, Ohio 43202. (Provides a program for use in schools; also a brochure describing various sexual abuse workshops.)

Audiovisuals to Use with Children

Boys Beware and *Girls Beware* (6–12 grades) (S)
  Films. Available from
AIMS Instructional Media, Inc.
626 Justin Avenue
Glendale, CA 91201

Child Abuse: Don't Hide the Hurt (school age) (M)
  Film. Available from
AIMS Instructional Media, Inc.
626 Justin Avenue
Glendale, CA 91201

For Pete's Sake, Tell! (school age) (S)
Speak Up, Say No! (school age) (S)
  Filmstrips. Available from
Krause House
P.O. Box 880
Oregon City, OR 97045

Negative Touch: Ways to Say No. (school age) (S)
  Film. Produced and distributed by
Child Abuse Series, Society for Visual Education
1345 Diversey Parkway
Chicago, IL 60614

No More Secrets (school age) (S)
  Film. Produced under grant from NCCAN
Distributed by ODN Productions
74 Varick Street
New York, NY 10013

Some Secrets Should Be Told (school age) (S)
Sometimes It's Okay to Tattle (school age) (S)
  Filmstrips. Produced by
Massachusetts Society for the Prevention of
Cruelty to Children
Distributed by
Family Information Systems
69 Clinton Road
Brookline, MA 02146

Who Do You Tell? (school age) (M)
  Film. Produced by J. Gary Mitchell Film Co.
Distributed by Coronet/MTI
108 Wilmot Road
Deerfield, IL 60015

Appendix J

Selected Materials

For Educators

Books

Ageton, Suzanne S. *Sexual Assault Among Adolescents*. Lexington, Mass.: D. C. Heath and Co., 1983

Aho, Jennifer Sowle, and Petras, John W. *Learning About Sexual Abuse*. Hillside, N.J.: Enslow Publishers (Bloy Street and Ramsey Avenue, Box 777, 07205), 1985.

American Association for Protecting Children. *Highlights of Official Child Neglect and Abuse Reporting, 1983*. Denver: American Humane Association, 1985.

Bass, Ellen, and Thornton, Louise, eds. *I Never Told Anyone: Writings by Women Survivors of Child Sexual Abuse*. New York: Harper and Row, 1983.

Burgess, Ann. *Child Pornography and Sex Rings*. Lexington, Mass.: Lexington Books, 1984.

Child Abuse and Development Disabilities: Essays. Essays from New England Regional Conference sponsored by United Cerebral Palsy of Rhode Island and United Cerebral Palsy Association, HEW. Washington, D.C.: Children's Bureau, Department of Health, Education and Welfare, 1980. No. OHDS 79–30226

"Child Sexual Abuse: Improving the System's Response." *Juvenile and Family Court Journal* 37, no. 2, 1986.

Child Welfare League of America. *Too Young to Run: The Status of Child Abuse in America*. New York: Child Welfare League of America, 1986. 12 pp.

Finkelhor, David. *Child Sexual Abuse*. New York: Free Press, 1984.

Forward, Susan, and Buck, Craig. *Betrayal of Innocence: Incest and Its Devastation*. New York: Penguin, 1979.

Garbarino, J.; Guttman, E.; and Seeley, J. W. *The Psychologically Battered Child*. San Francisco: Jossey Bass, 1986.

Garbarino, James, and Gilliam, Gwen. *Understanding Abusive Families*. Lexington, Mass.: Lexington Books, 1980.

Gil, David. *Violence Against Children: Physical Child Abuse in the United States*. Cambridge, Mass.: Harvard University Press, 1970.

Gil, Eliana. *Outgrowing the Pain: A Book for and About Adults Abused as Children*, 2d ed. San Francisco, Launch Press, 1984.

Horowitz, Robert M. *The Legal Rights of Children*. Monterey, Calif.: Shepard's McGraw-Hill, 1984.

Hyde, Margaret O. *Sexual Abuse: Let's Talk About It*. Philadelphia: Westminster Press, 1984.

Kempe, Ruth S., and Kempe, C. Henry. *The Common Secret: Sexual Abuse of Children and Adolescents*. New York: W. H. Freeman, 1984.

Kurtz, Howard. *The Beaten Victim*. Saratoga, Calif.: R & E. Publishers, 1983.

Lyon, E., and Cassady, L. "Speaking of Sex: Child Sexual Abuse Treatment and Team Development." Reprint from 94th Annual Convention of American Psychological Association, Washington, D.C., 1985.

Mayer, Adele. *Sexual Abuse: Cause, Consequences and Incestuous and Pedophilic Acts*. Holmes Beach, Fla.: Learning Publications, 1985.

_____. *Incest: A Treatment Manual for Therapy with Victims, Spouses and Offenders*. Holmes Beach, Fla.: Learning Publications, 1983.

Mrazek, Patricia B., and Kempe, C. Henry. *Sexually Abused Children and Their Families*. Oxford and New York: Pergamon Press, 1981.

National Center for Missing and Exploited Children. *Selected State Legislation: A Guide for Effective State Laws to Protect Children*. Washington, D.C.: National Center, 1985.

National Crime Prevention Council. *Keeping Kids Safe*. The Council, 733 15th Street, NW, Washington, DC 20005

National Committee for Prevention of Child Abuse. *Deaths Due to Maltreatment Soar*. Chicago: The Committee, 1987.

Nelson, Barbara J. *Making an Issue of Child Abuse: Political Agenda Setting for Social Problems*. Chicago: University of Chicago Press, 1984.

Nelson, Mary, and Clark, Kay, eds. *The Educator's Guide to Preventing Child Sexual Abuse*. Santa Cruz, Calif.: Newtwork Publications, 1986.

Olson, Marlys. "A Collaborative Approach to Prevention of Child Sexual Abuse." *Victimology: An International Journal* 10, nos. 1–4 (1985): 131–39.

Pelton, Leroy H., ed. *A Social Context of Child Abuse and Neglect*. New York: Human Sciences Press, 1981.

Polansky, N. *Child Neglect: Understanding and Reaching the Parent*. New York: Child Welfare League of America, 1972.

Porter, Ruth, ed. *Child Sexual Abuse Within the Family*. The Ciba Foundation. New York: Tavistock Publications, 1984.

Postman, Neil. *The Disappearance of Childhood*. New York: Dell, 1984.

Russell, Diana E. H. *The Secret Trauma: Incest in the Lives of Girls and Women*. New York: Basic Books, 1986.

_____. *Sexual Exploitation: Rape, Child Sexual Abuse and Workplace Harassment.* Los Angeles: Sage Publications, 1984.

Seattle Rape Relief. *Choices: Sexual Assault Prevention for Persons with Disabilities.* Seattle, Wash., 1985.

Soukup, Ruth; Wicker, Sharon; and Corbett, Joanne. *Three in Every Classroom.* Bemidji, Minn.: Sexual Assault Program, 1984. Distributed by Network Publications, Santa Cruz, CA.

Stacey, William A., and Shupe, Anson. *The Family Secret: Domestic Violence in America.* Boston: Beacon Press, n.d.

Summit, Roland C. "The Impact of Child Abuse: Psycho-Social and Educational Implications." In *Mental Health and the School*, edited by Sophia Leung. Oakbrook, Ill.: Eterna Press, 1986. (S)

_____. "Beyond Belief: The Reluctant Discovery of Incest." In *Women's Sexual Experience*, edited by Martha Kirkpatrick, pp. 127–50. New York and London: Plenum Press, 1982.

_____. "The Child Sexual Abuse Accommodation Syndrome." *Child Abuse and Neglect* 7 (1983): 177–93.

_____. "Recognition and Treatment of Child Sexual Abuse." In *Coping with Pediatric Illness*, edited by Charles Hollingsworth. New York: Spectrum Publications, 1983.

Summit, Roland C., and Krys, J. "Sexual Abuse of Children." *American Journal of Orthopsychiatry* 48, no. 2 (April 1978): 237–51.

Ten Bensel, R. W.; Arthur, L.; Brown, L.; and Riley, J. "Child Abuse and Neglect." *Juvenile and Family Court Journal* 35, no. 4 (Winter 1984–85).

Thorman, George. *Incestuous Families.* Springfield, Ill.: C. C. Thomas, 1983.

Weisberg, D. Kelly. *Children of the Night: A Study of Adolescent Prostitution.* Lexington, Mass.: Lexington Books, 1984.

Wooden, Ken. *Child Lures: A Guide for the Prevention of Molestation and Abduction.* Child Lures, 4345 Shelburne Road, Shelburne, VT 05482.

Government Pamphlets

The following can be obtained from the U.S. Government Printing Office, Washington, D.C.:

Child Pornography and Pedophilia. Parts I and II. 1985. S/N 052–070–06010–7 and 052–070–06019–1

An Educator's Role in the Prevention and Treatment of Child Abuse and Neglect, by Diane Broadhurst. Department of Health and Human Services. No. OHDS 84–30172

Perspectives on Child Maltreatment in the Mid '80s. Department of Health and Human Services, Human Development Series. No. OHDS 84–30338

A Research Report for Adults Who Work with Teenagers. 1985. S/N 017–024–01270

A Research Report for Teenagers. 1985. S/N 017–024–01259–9

Sexual Victimization of Adolescents. 1985. S/N 017–024–01239–4

Programs and Curricula

Child Sexual Abuse: What Your Children Should Know. Videocassette for adults. 90 min. Indiana University Audio-Visual Center, Bloomington, IN 47405.

Incest: Confronting the Silent Crime. Minnesota Program for Victims of Sexual Assault, State Documents Center, 117 University Avenue, St. Paul, MN 55155.

Preventing Sexual Abuse: Activities and Strategies for Those Working with Children and Adolescents, by Carol A. Plummer. Holmes Beach, Fla.: Learning Publications, 1984.

Sexual Abuse Prevention: A Lesson Plan, by Sandra L. Kleven. Coalition for Child Advocacy, P.O. Box 159, Bellingham, WA 98227.

Talking to Children—Talking to Parents About Sexual Assault. Lois Loontjens, King County Rape Relief, Distributed by Network Publications, P.O. Box 8506, Santa Cruz, CA 95061–8506.

Test Materials

The Child Abuse Potential Inventory Manual, 2d ed., by Joel S. Milner. Psytec, Inc., P.O. Box 300, Webster, NC 28788.

For Parents

Books

Adams, Caren; Fay, Jennifer; and Loreen-Martin, Jan. *No Is Not Enough: Helping Teenagers Avoid Sexual Assault.* San Luis Obispo, Calif.: Impact Publishers, 1984.

Bateman, Py, and Stringer, Gayle. *Where Do I Start? A Parent's Guide for Talking to Teens About Acquaintance Rape.* Seattle, Wash.: Alternatives to Fear, 1984.

Hechinger Grace. *How to Raise a Street Smart Child.* New York: Hechinger, 1984.

Hill, Eleanore. *The Family Secret: A Personal Account of Incest.* Santa Barbara, Calif.: Capra Press, 1985.

Hoff, P. M. *Parental Kidnapping: How to Prevent an Abduction and What to Do If Your Child Is Abducted.* Washington, D.C.: National Center for Missing and Exploited Children, 1985.

Kraiser, Sherryl L. *The Safe Child Book.* New York: Dell Publishing Co., 1985.

Windell, James, and Windell, Jill. *Understanding Runaways: A Parent's Guide to Adolescents Who Leave Home*. Washington, D.C.: Minerva Press (905 6th Street, SW, Suite 411, 20024), 1985.

For Children
Books for Young Children

Amerson, Ruth. *Hi! My Name Is Sissy*. Sanford, N.C.: Department of Social Services, 1984. (6 yrs.)

Berg, Eric. *Stop It!* Santa Cruz, Calif.: Network Publications, 1985.

―――. *Tell Someone!* Santa Cruz, Calif.: Network Publications, 1985.

―――. *Touch Talk!* Santa Cruz, Calif.: Network Publications, 1985.

Berry, Joy. *Alerting Kids to the Dangers of Sexual Abuse*. Waco, Tex.: Word, 1984.

Boehehold, Betty. *You Can Say "No": A Book About Protecting Yourself*. New York: Golden Books, 1985. (3–8 yrs.)

C.A.R.E. *Trust Your Feelings*. Surrey, B.C.: C.A.R.E. Productions, 1984.

Coalition for Child Advocacy. *Touching*. Bellingham, Wash.: Whatcom County Opportunity Council, 1985.

Davis, Diane. *Something Is Wrong at My House: A Book for Children About Domestic Violence*. Seattle, Wash.: Parenting Press, 1985. (4–12 yrs.)

Dayee, Frances S. *Safety Zone*. New York: Warner Books, 1984. (3–8 yrs.)

Ebert, Jeanne. *What Would You Do If . . . ? A Safety Game for You and Your Child*. Boston: Houghton Mifflin, 1985.

Ezrine, Linda. *Anna's Secret*. Baltimore, Md.: Harvey S. Spector Publishing Co., 1985.

Fassler, Joan. *The Boy with a Problem: Johnny Learns to Share His Troubles*. New York: Human Sciences Press, 1971. (4–8 yrs.)

Girard, Linda. *My Body Is Private*. Niles, Ill.: Whitman and Co., 1984. (3–8 yrs.)

Gordon, Sol, and Gordon, Judith. *A Better Safe Than Sorry Book: A Family Guide for Sexual Assault Prevention*. New York: Ed-U Press, 1984. (3–9 yrs.)

Joyce, Irma. *Never Talk to Strangers: A Book About Personal Safety*. New York: Western Publishing, 1985. (3–8 yrs.)

Lenett, Robin, and Crane, Bob. *It's O.K. to Say No: A Parent-Child Manual*. New York: Tor Books, 1985. Distributed by St. Martin's Press.

Mackey, Gene, and Swan, Helen. *The Wonder What Owl*, 1984.

Children's Institute of Kansas City, 9412 High Drive, Leawood, KS 66206. (3–7 yrs.)

Morgan, Marcia K. *My Feelings*. Eugene, Ore.: Equal Justice, 1984. Distributed by Network Publications, Santa Cruz, Calif.

Newman, Susan. *Never Say Yes to a Stranger: What Your Child Must Know to Stay Safe*. New York: Putnam Books, 1985.

Polese, Carolyn. *Promise Not to Tell*. New York: Human Sciences Press, 1985. (8 yrs. and up)

School Report Packet. Information on child abuse for K–8 students. Available from C. Henry Kempe National Center, 1205 Oneida Street, Denver, CO 80220.

Stanek, Muriel. *Don't Hurt Me, Mama*. Niles, Ill.: Whitman and Co., 1983. (6–9 yrs.)

Wachter, Oralee. *No More Secrets for Me*. Boston: Little Brown and Co., 1982. (3–12 yrs.)

Books for Adolescents

Adams, Caren, and Fay, Jennifer. *Nobody Told Me It Was Rape*. Santa Cruz, Calif.: Network Publications, 1984.

Austin Child Guidance and Evaluation Center. *Sexual Abuse: Information for Preteens and Teenagers*. Austin Child Guidance and Evalaution Center, 612 West 6th Street, Austin, TX 78701.

Bateman, Py. *So What If You're Not an Expert—You Can Still Take Steps to Protect Yourself Against Sexual Assault*. Seattle, Wash.: Alternatives to Fear, 1984.

Bateman, Py, and Mahoney, Bill. *Macho? What Do Girls Really Want?* Seattle, Wash.: Alternatives to Fear, 1985.

Fay, Jennifer, and Flerchinger, Billie Jo. *Top Secret*. Renton, Wash.: King County Rape Relief, 1982. (P.O. Box 1655, Fargo, ND 58107) (12–18 yrs.)

Mackey, Gene, and Swan, Helen. *Dear Elizabeth: Diary of an Adolescent Victim of Abuse*, 1983. Children's Institute of Kansas City, 9412 High Drive, Leawood, KS 66206. (13–18 yrs.)

McGovern, Kevin B. *Alice Doesn't Babysit Anymore*. Portland, Ore.: McGovern and Mulbacker Books, 1985.

Porteaus, Trace. *Let's Talk About Sexual Assault*. Victoria, B.C.: Women's Sexual Assault Center, 1984.

Research Paper Packet. Information on child abuse for high school through college students. Available from C. Henry Kempe National Center, 1205 Oneida Street, Denver, CO 80220.

Terkel, Susan Neiburg, and Rench, Janice E. *Feeling Safe, Feeling Strong*. Minneapolis: Lerner Publications, 1984. Distributed by Network Publications, Santa Cruz, Calif.

From Resource Organizations

The following materials are available from the organizations indicated:

American Public Welfare Association (APWA) (1125 15th Street, NW, Washington, DC 20005)

Characteristics of Children in Substitute and Adoptive Care: A Statistical Summary of the VCIS National Child Welfare Data Base, December 1983. (120 pp.)

Child Protective Service Intervention with the Sexually Victimized Child, September 1980. (20 pp.)

Cultural Responsiveness in Child Protective Services, December 1979. (10 pp.)

Dealing with Issues of Confidentiality in Child Protective Services, July 1979. (7 pp.)

A *Guide to Delivery of Child Protective Services*, September 1981. (240 pp.)

Improving Child Protective Services Through the Use of Multidisciplinary Teams, June 1981. (18 pp.)

Reference Guide to Child Abuse and Neglect Materials Available from States and Counties, 2d ed., September 1981. (31 pp.)

A *Survey of the Use and Functioning of Multidisciplinary Teams in Child Protective Services*, September 1981. (30 pp.)

Terminating Child Protective Service Cases, May 1979. (9 pp.)

Worker Burnout in Child Protective Services, October 1979. (7 pp.)

Childhelp USA (6463 Independence Avenue, Woodland Hills, CA 91367)

He Said He Loved Mom, but . . .

How Could Momma Say She Loved Us . . .

I Wasn't Too Young at Sixteen

No One Knew My Secret 'Til One Day . . .

The Home and School Institute, Inc. (Special Projects Office, 1201 16th Street, NW, Washington, DC 20036)

Bright Idea (Guidance and Family Learning) (Preschool–6)

Families Learning Together (Family Learning and Basic Skills) (K–6)

Get Smart: Advice for Teens with Babies (7–12)

Survival Guide for Busy Parents: Help Children Do Well at School While You Do Well on the Job (K–6)

Kidsrights (401 South Highland, Mount Dora, FL 32757)

Abuse and Neglect, by Joy Berry (6–10 yrs.)

Adolescent Abuse and Neglect, by K. K. Hirayama (training package)

Child Abuse—Is It Happening to You? by Bridget Wakehter (3–8 yrs.)

Feelings—Everybody Has Them: Comprehensive Activity Book, by Stephanie Neuman (5–10 yrs.)

Kids Go to Court Too: What You Will See and Do, Hennepin County (Minnesota) Attorney's Office (3–8 yrs.)

A Little Bird Told Me About... My Feelings, by Marcia K. Morgan (4–10 yrs.)

Mothers and Others Be Aware: My Daughter from Baby Dolls to Daddy's Doll, by Donna Miller

No Is Not Enough: Helping Teenagers Avoid Sexual Assault, by Caren Adams and Jennifer Fay (10–17 yrs.) (S)

Protect Your Child from Sexual Abuse: A Parent's Guide, by Janie Hart-Rossi (S)

Respond: Teaching Children Self-Protection, by J. Anderson and J. Benson

Sexual Abuse, Let's Talk About It, by Margaret O. Hyde (10–17 yrs.) (S)

Some Questions You May Ask About Going to Court... and Some Answers That Will Help You, by Kate Hubbard and Evelyn Berlin (8–13 yrs.)

Speaking Out (video) (9–13 yrs.)

Spiderman and Power Pack, National Center for Prevention of Child Abuse and Marvel Comics (7–14 yrs.) (S)

The Talking and Telling About Touching Game, by Thomas G. Beck (all ages) (S)

Talking to Children—Talking to Parents About Sexual Assault, by Jennifer Fay (S)

Your Child's Self-Esteem, by Dorothy Corkille Briggs

National Clearinghouse on Child Abuse and Neglect Research and Information (NCCAN, Children's Bureau, Department of Health and Human Services, P.O. Box 1182, Washington, DC 20013)

Child Abuse and Neglect: An Informed Approach to a Shared Concern, 1986.

Child Neglect: A Selected Annotated Bibliography, 1985.

Immunity to Reporters' Laws Concerning Child Abuse and Neglect, 1986.

Teachers and Child Abuse and Neglect, 1986.

Who Must Report Laws Concerning Child Abuse and Neglect, 1986.

Bibliography

1. Adams, C., and Fay, J. *Nobody Told Me It Was Rape*. Santa Cruz: Network Publications, 1984.

2. Allen, Charlotte Vale. *Daddy's Girl*. New York: Wyndham Books, 1981.

3. Brady, Katherine. *Father's Days: A True Story of Incest*. New York: Seaview Books, 1979.

4. Broadhurst, Diane. *Educators, Schools and Child Abuse*. Washington, D.C.: National Committee for Prevention of Child Abuse, 1986.

5. Burgess, Ann Wolbert; Groth, A. Nicholas; Halstrom, Lynda Lytle; and Sgroi, Suzanne M. *Sexual Assault of Children and Adolescents*. Lexington, Mass.: Lexington Books, 1978.

6. Cantwell, Hendrika. "Neglect: Responses and Solutions." Minicourse presented at Seventh National Conference on Child Abuse and Neglect, Chicago, November 10–13, 1985.

7. Castillo, Gloria A. *Left-Handed Teaching: Lessons in Affective Education*. New York: Praeger Publishing, 1974.

8. Caulfield, Barbara. *The Legal Aspects of Protective Services for Abused and Neglected Children*. Washington, D.C.: U.S. Department of Health, Education and Welfare, 1978.

9. Chalmers, Mary Jane. "The Murder of Robbie Wayne, Age Six." *Reader's Digest*, November 1980.

10. Child Welfare League of America. *Too Young to Run: The Status of Child Abuse in America*. New York: Child Welfare League of America, 1986.

11. Christiansen, James. *Educational and Psychological Problems of Abused Children*. Saratoga, Calif.: Century 21 Publishing Co., 1980.

12. Collins, Marva, and Tamarkin, Civia. *Marva Collins' Way*. Los Angeles: J. P. Tarcher, 1982.

13. Davis, James R. *Help Me, I'm Hurt: The Child Abuse Handbook*. Dubuque, Iowa: Kendall/Hunt Publishing Co., 1982.

14. DeFrancis, Vincent. *Protecting the Child Victim of Sex Crimes Committed by Adults: Final Report*. Denver, Colo.: American Humane Association, 1968.

15. Denker, Henry. *The Scofield Diagnosis*. New York: Simon and Schuster, 1977.

16. Finkelhor, David. "What's Wrong with Sex Between Children and Adults?" *American Journal of Orthopsychiatry* 49, no. 4 (October 1979): 692–97.

17. _____. *Sexually Victimized Children*. New York: Free Press, 1979.

18. _____. *Child Sexual Abuse*. New York: Free Press, 1984.

19. Fisher, B.; Berdie, J.; Cook, J.; and Day, N. *Adolescent Abuse and Neglect: Intervention Strategies*. Washington, D.C.: U.S. Department of Health and Human Services, 1980.

20. Fontana, Vincent J. *Somewhere a Child Is Crying: Maltreatment—Causes and Prevention*. New York: Mentor Books, New American Library, 1973.

21. Giovannoni, Jeanne M., and Becerra, Rosina M. *Defining Child Abuse*. New York: Free Press, 1979.

22. Goldstein, Joseph; Freud, Anna; and Solnit, Albert J. *Beyond the Best Interests of the Child*. New York: Free Press, 1973.

23. Gray, E., and Di Leonardi, J. *Evaluating Child Abuse Prevention Programs*. Chicago: National Committee for Prevention of Child Abuse, 1982.

24. Groth, A. Nicholas. "The Incest Offender." In *Handbook of Clinical Intervention in Child Sexual Abuse*, edited by Suzanne Sgroi. Lexington, Mass.: Lexington Books, 1982.

25. Hally, Carolyn; Polansky, Nancy F.; Polansky, Norman A. *Child Neglect Mobilizing Services*. Washington, D.C.: U.S. Department of Health and Human Services, 1980.

26. Helfer, Ray E. *Childhood Comes First: A Crash Course in Childhood for Adults*. East Lansing, Mich.: Ray E. Helfer, 1978.

27. _____, and Kempe, C. Henry. *Child Abuse: The Family and the Community*. Cambridge, Mass.: Ballinger Publishing Co., 1976.

28. Howe, Leland W., and Howe, Mary Martha. *Personalizing Education: Values Clarification and Beyond*. New York: Hart Publishing Co., 1975.

29. Justice, Blair, and Justice, Rita. *The Broken Taboo: Sex in the Family*. New York: Human Sciences Press, 1979.

30. Justice, Rita, and Justice, Blair. *The Abusing Family*. New York: Human Sciences Press, 1976.

31. Katz, Sanford N. *When Parents Fail: The Law's Response to Family Breakdown*. Boston, Mass.: Beacon Press, 1971.

32. Kempe, C. Henry, and Helfer, Ray E. *Helping the Battered Child and His Family*. New York: Lippincott, 1972.

33. Knight, Michael E. *Teaching Children to Love Themselves.* Englewood Cliffs, N.J.: Prentice-Hall, 1982.

34. Landau, Hortense R.; Salus, Marsha K.; Stiffarm, Thelma; with Kalb, Nora Lee. *Child Protection: The Role of the Courts.* Washington, D.C.: U.S. Department of Health and Human Services, 1980.

35. Leavitt, Jerome E. *The Battered Child: Selected Readings.* Fresno, Calif.: California State University, 1974.

36. Martin, Harold P. *Treatment for Abused and Neglected Children.* Washington, D.C.: U.S. Department of Health, Education and Welfare, 1979.

37. Meiselman, Karin C. *Incest.* San Francisco, Calif.: Jossey-Bass, 1978.

38. Niatove, Connie. "Arts Therapy with Sexually Abused Children." In *Handbook of Clinical Intervention in Child Sexual Abuse,* edited by Suzanne Sgroi. Lexington, Mass.: Lexington Books, 1982.

39. Polansky, Norman A.; Chalmers, Mary Ann; Buttenweiser, Elizabeth; and Williams, David P. *Damaged Parents: An Anatomy of Child Neglect.* Chicago: University of Chicago Press, 1981.

40. Ragan, Cynthia.; Salus, Marsha K.; and Schutze, Gretchen. *Child Protection: Providing Ongoing Services.* Washington, D.C.: U.S. Department of Health and Human Services, 1980.

41. Russell, Diana. *The Secret Trauma.* New York: Basic Books, 1986.

42. Sanford, Linda Tschinhart. *The Silent Children: A Parent's Guide to the Prevention of Child Sexual Abuse.* Garden City, N.Y.: Anchor Press/Doubleday, 1980.

43. *Sexual Abuse of Children: Selected Readings.* Washington, D.C.: U.S. Department of Health and Human Services, 1980 (#78–30161).

44. Sgroi, Suzanne, ed. *Handbook of Clinical Intervention in Child Sexual Abuse.* Lexington, Mass.: Lexington Books, 1982.

45. Stember, Clara Jo. "Art Therapy: A New Use in the Diagnosis and Treatment of Sexually Abused Children." In *Sexual Abuse of Children: Selected Readings.* Washington, D.C.: U.S. Department of Health and Human Services, 1980 (#78-30161).

46. Tower, Cynthia Crosson. "Secret Scars: A Handbook for the Adult Survivor of Child Sexual Abuse." Unpublished manuscript, 1985.

47. Walters, David R. *Physical and Sexual Abuse of Children:*

Causes and Treatment. Bloomington, Ind.: Indiana University Press, 1975.

48. Wells, Harold C., and Canfield, Jack. *One Hundred Ways to Enhance Self-Concepts in the Classroom: Handbook for Teachers and Parents*. Englewood Cliffs, N.J.: Prentice-Hall, 1976.

49. Williams, Linda V. *Teaching for the Two-Sided Mind*. Englewood Cliffs, N.J.: Prentice-Hall, 1983.

50. Young, Leontine. *Wednesday's Children: A Study of Child Neglect and Abuse*. New York: McGraw-Hill Book Co., 1964.

DATE DUE

OCT 11 '94	MAR 0 8 1998	
OCT 14	MAR 0 8 1998	
DEC 3 '94	APR 2 6 1998	
NOV 2 9	APR 1 6 1998	
FEB 2 2 1995	JUL 2 8 1998	
APR 0 5 1995	JUL 1 6 1998	
MAR 2 0 1995		
APR 2 7 1995		
APR 0 4		
OCT 2 4 1995		
OCT 3 1 1995		
DEC 0 3 1995		
DEC 11 1995		
APR 0 3 1996		
APR 3 0 1996		
APR 1 1 1996		
JUL 2 9 1997		